IN THE
NATIONAL INTEREST

General Sir John Monash once exhorted a graduating class to 'equip yourself for life, not solely for your own benefit but for the benefit of the whole community'. At the university established in his name, we repeat this statement to our own graduating classes, to acknowledge how important it is that common or public good flows from education.

Universities spread and build on the knowledge they acquire through scholarship in many ways, well beyond the transmission of this learning through education. It is a necessary part of a university's role to debate its findings, not only with other researchers and scholars, but also with the broader community in which it resides.

Publishing for the benefit of society is an important part of a university's commitment to free intellectual inquiry. A university provides civil space for such inquiry by its scholars, as well as for investigations by public intellectuals and expert practitioners.

This series, In the National Interest, embodies Monash University's mission to extend knowledge and encourage informed debate about matters of great significance to Australia's future.

Professor Margaret Gardner AC
President and Vice-Chancellor,
Monash University

ANDREW LEIGH

FAIR GAME: LESSONS FROM SPORT FOR A FAIRER SOCIETY & A STRONGER ECONOMY

MONASH
UNIVERSITY
PUBLISHING

Monash University Publishing
Matheson Library Annexe
40 Exhibition Walk
Monash University
Clayton, Victoria 3800, Australia
https://publishing.monash.edu

Monash University Publishing brings to the world publications which advance the best traditions of humane and enlightened thought.

ISBN: 9781922633477 (paperback)
ISBN: 9781922633491 (ebook)

Series: In the National Interest
Editor: Louise Adler
Project manager & copyeditor: Paul Smitz
Designer: Peter Long
Typesetter: Cannon Typesetting
Proofreader: Gillian Armitage
Printed in Australia by Ligare Book Printers

A catalogue record for this book is available from the National Library of Australia.

FAIR GAME: LESSONS FROM SPORT FOR A FAIRER SOCIETY & A STRONGER ECONOMY

In 1945, Australian batsman Graham Williams strode onto the pitch at Lord's Cricket Ground in London. A former Sheffield Shield player, he had only been released from a prisoner-of-war camp two weeks earlier. Williams was emaciated, having spent almost four years of World War II in captivity after his plane was shot down over Libya. As he walked onto the ground, he turned his head from side to side, taking in the scene, still struggling to believe where he was.

And then the applause started. As one, the English crowd rose to its feet and clapped. It wasn't the sound of a crowd admiring a great sporting accomplishment. It was the noise of 30 000 people honouring an athlete. Recalling the moment decades later, one fellow cricketer said: 'I have heard people clapping at Lord's many times ... But this was applause with a difference. It was muffled and ongoing. Everybody stayed standing as he walked and continued this beautiful, hushed applause ...

I often think what a marvellous piece of music that kind of applause would make … Beethoven could have put it to something stunning.[1]

Sport can bring out our finest qualities. The people of Lithgow were so enamoured of sprinter Marjorie Jackson that they built a cinder track for her to train on. They also helped raise funds so she could attend the 1952 Helsinki Olympics, where she won Australia's first ever women's athletic gold medals in the 100 metres and 200 metres. When Jackson returned home by train, the woman they named 'the Lithgow Flash' could hear her fans cheering before she could even see the local station.[2]

At its best, sport embodies both achievement and egalitarianism. We admire athletes who perform new feats of strength, speed and dexterity. We prize the idea that what matters isn't their bank balances or their connections but their hard work—like Jackson's willingness to train through the fog and sleet of a Lithgow winter. In team sports, we want to see a tournament in which the last-placed team of one season starts the following year with a fighting chance of winning.

This dual nature of sport has also provided memorable markers on Australia's reconciliation journey: the Indigenous cricket team that toured England in 1868; the success of Cathy Freeman in the 400 metres at the 2000 Sydney Olympics; Johnathan Thurston captaining the North Queensland Cowboys to their first National Rugby League (NRL) premiership in 2015; Ash Barty becoming tennis's world number one in 2019. Many white Australians who grew up in rural areas say that their first friendships with Indigenous people were forged on the playing field.

Sport is a source of national and personal pride for millions. Watch an international sporting competition and there's a reasonable chance an Aussie will be in contention. Every year, through a combination of ingenuity, grit and teamwork, Australians smash records like plates at a Greek wedding. But sport isn't purely an elite activity. For millions of Australians, participating in sport is integral to a good life. Whether it's a hit of tennis, a gym workout or a dance session, exercise is part of a life well lived. As the father of three sons, my favourite moments with them are when we're physically active: cycling down a mountain, bodysurfing a wave, or just chatting while we walk the dog. My wife Gweneth and I both notice that, after they've done some exercise, our boys are nicer people to be around: funnier, kinder, less inclined to squabble. That's true of their parents too.

Yet the Australian economy hasn't produced the same kinds of gold-medal-winning performances and individual satisfaction. Productivity—the amount that each worker produces in an hour—is barely rising. The nation's biggest companies today are virtually identical to those that dominated our economy in the 1980s, and not all that much changed from the behemoths of the 1910s. Megafirms are merging like never before, while the new business startup rate has dropped. Other measures of economic dynamism are deteriorating. Switching jobs usually produces big productivity gains for companies and significant wage gains for workers. But the job-switching rate has declined. The same goes for geographic mobility: Australians are less likely to move house now than in the past.

Unlike the egalitarian ethos that shapes the best sporting contests, the Australian economy is delivering an increasing share of the gains to a fortunate few. From 1975 to 2021, real wages grew by 33 per cent for the lowest-paid, 55 per cent for median earners and 81 per cent for the highest-paid.[3] The number of billionaires ballooned from zero in 1986 to 137 in 2022. Australians now have fewer friends, join fewer organisations, and are less likely to volunteer.[4] The rise of inequality and the decline of community means that Australia is increasingly becoming a nation that values 'me' over 'we'.

At a time when the social divides that separate Australians are wider than ever, sport can provide a common language and a shared experience. Many people who have migrated to Melbourne have found that picking an Australian Football League (AFL) team is as essential as knowing where to catch a tram. In the Victorian capital, Aussie Rules provides a common language that often helps to bridge differences in ethnicity, class or culture. In Townsville, Rugby League plays a similar role. When floods hit the North Queensland town in 2019, no-one was surprised to see Cowboys players helping evacuate stranded residents.

Whether in the stadium or in front of the television, Australians are enthusiastic fans with a larrikin spirit.

When a cricket match lags, a Mexican wave often begins to make its way around the ground, with spectators cajoling those who fail to jump to their feet. On the day Australia won the America's Cup in 1983, then prime minister Bob Hawke spontaneously announced a national holiday to celebrate the yachting victory, declaring: 'Any boss who sacks anyone today for not turning up is a bum.' During their commentary on the Sydney Olympics, comedy duo Roy and HG created an unofficial games mascot—Fatso the Fat-Arsed Wombat—which became so popular that a statue was erected in its honour at Sydney Olympic Park.

This love of impish larks and a disdain for officialdom explain the affinity that many people have with swimmer Dawn Fraser, who won the 100-metres freestyle at three successive Olympics, before receiving a ten-year ban from the Australian Amateur Swimming Association for stealing a Japanese flag as a prank. Fifty-seven years later, the Sport Australia Hall of Fame introduced the 'Dawn Award' for athletes 'who are courageous, brave, and have changed sport for the better'. That willingness to challenge the dusty conventional wisdom isn't just vital in sport—it's fundamental to forging an economy where the quality of an idea matters more than the status of the person proposing it.

SPORTING TRAGICS

Like many Australians, I'm a sporting tragic. In my case, I trace the passion back to my grandfather, Keith Leigh, a Melbourne Methodist church minister who loved distance running. To celebrate his fiftieth birthday, Keith ran 50 miles (80 kilometres) from his home in Rosanna in Melbourne's north-east, all the way to Mount Dandenong to see his mother at a retirement home, then back again. Keith loved the freedom of running, and the time it gave him to cogitate on his sermons and pastoral duties. He died in 1970, aged fifty-eight, while doing a run up kunanyi / Mount Wellington in Hobart to raise money for overseas aid.

My father Michael Leigh was also a marathon runner who grew up watching Ron Clarke, Herb Elliott and John Landy. My favourite photograph of my father and grandfather has them both lacing up their running shoes, big goofy grins on their faces. Over recent years, I've had the chance to follow in their fleet footsteps, racing the six World Marathon Majors—in Tokyo, Berlin, Chicago, New York, London and Boston—as a supporter of the Indigenous Marathon Foundation. I've run more than a dozen sub-3-hour marathons, and even managed to win the local Canberra bush marathon. I've run a 100-kilometre trail race. I've completed an Ironman triathlon which involved a 3.8-kilometre swim, a 180-kilometre cycle and a 42.2-kilometre run, and required 2–3 hours a day of training in the months leading up to the event.

My typical day starts with an hour-long run in the bush reserve behind our house, where I'll nod to the kangaroos, smile at the kookaburras and admire the sunrise. If I've pushed hard—with hill repetitions or a sprint session—it gives me the satisfaction of knowing that the rest of the day will be comparatively easy. As the saying goes, if you swallow a live frog in the morning, nothing else you do will be the toughest thing of the day.

I'm not delusional—a middle-aged runner like me is hardly in the league of those who dominate track and road races. But I get pleasure from sweating hard, and joy from training with people who are quicker than me. Races are both an incentive to train and a chance to test yourself. They're also fun: if you're not smiling when you cross the finish line, you're not doing it right. Running is an ideal way of exploring a new city or unwinding after a rough day. It's cheaper than snowboarding, healthier than croquet, safer than rock climbing and easier than skydiving.

Why is sport so important to Australians? One reason is our environment. Perth and Brisbane get almost twice as many hours of sunshine as Paris and Berlin. Most Australian cities are spared the snowstorms of Europe and North America, don't cop the stifling humidity of Africa and South-East Asia, and aren't plagued by the air pollution that chokes cities elsewhere on the globe. We could always use more sporting facilities, but thousands of ovals, tennis courts and swimming pools are dotted across our suburbs and towns. All up, Australia is a pretty good place to be active.

Any discussion of sport has to recognise its imperfections, both at the elite and local levels. It used to be said that the captain of the Australian cricket team was the most important role after the prime minister.

If that's true, then it's an irony that the era since 2010 has seen a rapid turnover in both prime ministers (Kevin Rudd, Julia Gillard, Kevin Rudd, Tony Abbott, Malcolm Turnbull, Scott Morrison, Anthony Albanese) and cricket captains (Ricky Ponting, Michael Clarke, Shane Watson, Steve Smith, Tim Paine, Pat Cummins), with, in the latter category, Smith being fired after a ball-tampering scandal and Paine quitting after a sexting incident. Problems that afflict elite sport, including sexism, racism, homophobia, excessive alcohol consumption and violence, are all present in community contests, with amateurs sometimes copying the bad behaviour of professionals.

It's also worth noting that, over the first two decades of the twenty-first century, there was a drop in the share of Australians playing organised sport.[5] Two-thirds of Australian adults are overweight or obese—significantly above the average for rich nations. The average Australian woman today weighs about the same as the average man did in the 1960s.[6] The physical prowess of Australian children is also falling short. Asked to do a standing jump, the typical year 6 child in the current era will jump 17 centimetres less than year 6 students a generation ago.[7]

Still, Australia currently produces a remarkable number of world-beating athletes, including cyclists, cricketers and canoe sprinters—to pick just one letter of the alphabet. Australia will also host the 2032 Olympics in Brisbane, after previously hosting the games in 1956 and 2000. The world's premier sporting contest comes to Australia about one time in ten—a remarkable fact when you consider that we comprise just 0.3 per cent of the world's population.

And while sport isn't life, it provides crucial life lessons. Training lays the groundwork for success. Stress is no excuse for bad behaviour. Respect your opponents. Everyone makes mistakes—it's how you react that counts. Luck matters. Teams are greater than the sum of their parts. Win with dignity. Lose with integrity.

In sport, equal treatment is fundamental. Teams playing at an outdoor venue swap ends at half-time so that neither side gets the benefit of a tailwind. Martial arts fighters are matched by weight to ensure a fair fight. Amateur golf events and many professional horse races use a handicap system. In team sports, player drafts, salary caps and revenue-sharing are imposed to ensure that no team monopolises a tournament.

There's even something called the Köhler effect, when athletes perform better as part of a team than when they're racing as individuals. A study of swimmers in the 2008 Beijing Olympics found that, when they raced in a relay, their times improved by half a per cent. That's a substantial impact in a sport where races are determined by hundredths of a second.[8] If you've ever trained harder in a gym class than when working out solo, or pushed yourself further in a team training session than when on your own, you've benefited from the Köhler effect.

Sport isn't utopia, but for all its flaws, it has much to teach us about creating a fairer society and a stronger economy. When he was inducted into the Sport Australia

Hall of Fame on 10 December 1985, Australia's greatest cricketer, Don Bradman, summed up his views on the relationship between success and decency:

> When considering the stature of an athlete—or for that matter any person—I set great store on certain qualities which I believe to be essential in addition to skill. They are that the person conducts his or her life with dignity, with integrity, with courage, and perhaps most of all with modesty. These virtues are totally compatible with pride, ambition and competitiveness.

Sport teaches us that we don't have to sacrifice egalitarianism and honour in pursuit of victory.

FASTER, HIGHER, STRONGER

If you had to jump over a high metal bar, how would you do it? If it was low enough, you might try hurdling it. If there was something soft on the other side to land on, you might try diving over it, or even jumping sideways, scissoring your legs to clear it. For decades, this pretty much summed up how high jumpers, from schoolchildren to world champions, approached the sport. Then came Dick Fosbury.

Born in 1947 in Portland, Oregon, the lanky Fosbury began trialling alternative ways of high jumping when he was sixteen years old—around the time that sports administrators were changing the landing pits, replacing the woodchips and sand with bundles of foam rubber. Fosbury's early attempts have been described as an 'airborne seizure', but his experimentation eventually led him to an entirely new technique whereby he cleared the bar by hurling himself backwards, head first, and flicking his legs up at the end. In the 1968 Mexico City Olympics, Fosbury put his new technique on show and won gold. At the next Olympics, a majority of high jumpers used his method. Today, the Fosbury flop is used by virtually every serious high jumper.

Other sports have been revolutionised by an athletic innovator. The nineteenth-century cricketer Christina Willes found that the game's conventional underarm bowling action was impeded by her wide skirt. So Willes took to bowling overarm, an approach that was copied by her brother and other men, and finally made legal in 1835.[9] The gymnast Simone Biles has four gymnastic elements named after her, including a double-twisting double-tucked salto backwards dismount off the balance beam—a dazzling move that led to a dispute with the International Gymnastics Federation over whether its rating should take into account the potential for gymnasts to land on their neck. Biles is the only woman to have completed in competition a Yurchenko double pike, in which she enters the vault with a roundoff back handspring, drives her feet hard into the springboard, uses her hands to propel herself off the vaulting table, and then spins two-and-a-half times in the air before landing on her feet. One of the hardest aspects of the manoeuvre is that, as she spins, Biles is in an L-shaped 'pike' position—at its highest point, she is nearly 3 metres off the ground.

Technology has changed sports in unexpected ways. In 1877, rower Ned Trickett astonished the crowd along the Parramatta River when he used a scull with a sliding seat to defeat reigning world champion Michael Rush. In 1983, Australia won the America's Cup by using a yacht with a winged keel, the first successful challenge to the Americans in 132 years. In other contexts, innovations have been outlawed for the sake of making a sport safer or fairer. Formula One banned anti-lock braking and traction control in 1994. Swimming banned bodysuits in 2010. Distance running banned shoe soles thicker than 4 centimetres in 2020. And virtually all sports ban performance-enhancing drugs.

Sporting innovation is how sporting records keep falling. Today's elite athletes have better equipment, better nutrition and better coaching than those of past generations. Competitors start training at a younger age, and they train harder than ever before. In some instances, this has produced remarkable improvements. No-one in history had run a 4-minute mile until 1954. Today, more than a dozen high-school students have managed the feat. In 1950, the bench press world record was 181 kilograms. Now, it is 355 kilograms. Since 1908, the marathon world record has fallen from 2 hours and 55 minutes to 2 hours and 1 minute. To put this into perspective, an amateur runner like me could have won the 1908 London Olympic marathon, but I wouldn't be able to keep up with

Eliud Kipchoge, the current world-record holder, for more than a few hundred metres.

Over the long sweep of history, Australia's economy has gotten much stronger, too. This is largely thanks to something called labour productivity. Australian workers today produce seven times as much every hour as they did in 1901.[10] Productivity explains almost all of the increase in national income since Federation, and virtually all of the growth in real wages. Thanks to productivity growth, the buying power of a worker's daily pay packet is now bigger than the weekly pay packet of a worker at the time of Federation. One way to see this is by calculating how long the typical person must work to afford certain items.[11] Since 1901, the amount of work required to buy a simple bicycle has dropped from 527 hours to 8 hours. The amount of work required to buy 1 kilogram of rump steak has dropped from 143 minutes to 38 minutes. The time cost of a litre of milk has declined from 31 minutes to 2 minutes.

Productivity is sometimes associated with working harder, but it's really about working smarter. If an office employee can write a high-quality report in half as many hours as their co-worker, then that means they are twice as productive. Another myth about productivity is that it leads to more stuff and therefore to more pollution. But when people are working in service industries, productivity is often about creating knowledge or experiences. There's no reason why making offices more efficient should trash the planet.

Productivity doesn't automatically bring fairness. In recent times, workers haven't received their fair share of the modest productivity growth delivered by the economy. But without rising productivity, wages will eventually stagnate and living standards will stop increasing. Whether your priority is longer life spans or lower taxes, raising social security benefits or building freeways, you should be in favour of productivity growth. Productivity is the economic equivalent of fitness.

Unfortunately, Australia's economic fitness plan has turned flabby. Labour productivity grew at around 2 per cent a year from the 1970s to the early 2010s, but from 2015–16 to 2020–21 it grew at less than 1 per cent—well below the historical average. And the cost to incomes is clear. The decade ending 2020 saw the slowest rate of growth in income per person of any decade in the post–World War II era.[12] In the years before COVID hit, economic growth had slowed. Wage growth was tepid. Construction and business investment were languishing.

While our best athletes have been setting world records, our best companies have been falling behind their global peers.[13] Since 2002, the most productive Australian firms (the top 5 per cent) have grown about half as fast as the most productive firms globally. The best of 'Made in Australia' hasn't kept pace with the best of 'Made in Germany', 'Made in the Netherlands' or 'Made in America'.

A similar problem afflicts 'high-growth firms'— companies growing at a rate of more than 20 per cent a year.[14] These dynamic organisations account for a majority of all economic activity. Like a rapidly improving teenage athlete, they're constantly hitting new benchmarks. And just as healthy teens are constantly getting smarter and stronger, high-growth firms account for a massive share of innovation and research. Yet, in the first two decades of the twenty-first century, the share of high-growth firms in the economy declined significantly.

We need to be careful to avoid complacency. In his book *The Australian Miracle*, biologist Thomas Barlow pointed out that the oft-cited list of national discoveries— the black box, polymer banknote, Hills hoist, wine cask, two-stroke lawnmower and so on—is no more than should be expected of a country our size. Australians are an inventive people, but it would be arrogant to think that our ingenuity places us far ahead of the Swiss, Canadians or New Zealanders. Take a moment to look around you now and ask yourself how many of the products you see were invented by Australians. Unless you're reading this book on a farm, the answer is likely to be 'Not many'. As Donald Horne's *Lucky Country* warned, there is a risk that we 'live on other people's ideas' rather than coming up with our own.

And then there's the lack of new companies. For all the talk of Australia as a 'startup nation', the country's new business creation rate isn't accelerating. In fact, it seems to be stopping, having fallen substantially during the first two decades of the twenty-first century.[15] In this period, firms became increasingly likely to fail. For all the talk of incubators, accelerators and innovation, our nation isn't starting as many businesses as it used to.

Australia is also failing to foster startup talent across the community. On average, startup founders are most likely to be young men from affluent backgrounds. This isn't just inequitable, it's also inefficient. Society ends up missing out on the productive talents of potential Elizabeth Blackburns (molecular biologist and Nobel prize winner) and Melanie Perkinses (co-founder of Canva) merely because talent springs up in an unexpected place.

Talent identification is a challenge in sport, too. In 1988, the Australian Institute of Sport tested hundreds of teenagers in Canberra and Queanbeyan schools. One student, Megan Still, had never been in a rowing scull before. Every time she pulled the oars, she unbalanced the boat, but it was because she was exerting an unusually large amount of power.[16] The coaches put their unconventional rower into a talent-identification program. Eight years later, Still and her rowing partner Kate Slatter became the first Australian women to win an Olympic gold medal in the sport.

There's good reason to think that talent identification is more effective in sport than entrepreneurship. In the United States, children born into the top 1 per cent of the income distribution are ten times as likely to become inventors as those born into the bottom half.[17] Similarly, in Australia, the children of entrepreneurial parents are over-represented among innovators.[18] Women comprise just 22 per cent of founders. And because most entrepreneurs make a personal cash contribution to kickstart their business, family money helps. Not everyone realises their luck. As the baseball saying goes: 'Some people are born on third base and go through life thinking they hit a triple.' If Australia wants more startups, we need to start talent-scouting entrepreneurship in poor communities with the same zeal with which sporting teams identify and resource promising young players.

When a sporting team wants to improve, it often looks to bring in ideas from its rivals. In 1974, the Parramatta Eels finished at the bottom of the NRL ladder. So the following year, they hired Norm Provan, who had taken St George to four premierships as its captain-coach. That year, Parramatta reached the finals, earning Provan the title 'team rebuilder'. Over the next decade, Parramatta became one of the leading clubs in the league. Fans sometimes criticise players or coaches for switching teams, but the whole sport benefits from the diffusion of training techniques and game strategies. If you love the game, you should love it when players and coaches switch teams.

Much the same is true for the economy. Workers who come in from outside bring new ideas and fresh perspectives. As a result, workers who switch jobs typically experience a significant pay increase. If your friends are grumbling about their salary, the best advice you can give them is to get an outside job offer. And just as shackling a player to a team tends to be bad for the sport, less job-switching means less wage growth. While changing jobs tends to benefit workers, it is happening less often than in past decades. Forget what you've read about a fast-churning labour market and the end of 'jobs for life'. Workers are staying in their jobs for longer. In the early 2000s, the rate of job-switching was 11 per cent a year; two decades on, it's down to 8 per cent.[19] It's not the fault of employees; it's simply that fewer good opportunities are available. With fewer startups, it stands to reason there are fewer startup jobs.

Job mobility isn't the only form of mobility that's declined. For every five people who moved interstate in the 1970s, only four did the same in the 2010s.[20] Figures on within-state movement show a similar pattern.[21] Australians today are more likely to stick to one spot than in the past. Sometimes it's good to stay put—you get to know your neighbours, and you're able to build a stronger sense of community. But mobility also brings diversity and new ideas, providing cities and regions with fresh perspectives. There's a reason why many budding tennis players move to Florida, runners to Kenya's Rift Valley, karate fighters to Okinawa and rock climbers to Yosemite. These locations provide ideal physical environments for training and allow them to work with the world's best to hone their specialised talents. Like job mobility, geographic mobility is a key part of a dynamic economy. Yet the latest figures suggest that today's Australians are slower to move location than generations past.

The stagnation even extends to the sharemarket.[22] In the mid-1980s, the largest US firms were IBM, Mobil, Exxon, Ford and General Motors. Today, they are Apple,

Microsoft, Alphabet, Amazon and Tesla. In Australia, however, there's been barely any change. In the mid-1980s, the largest Australian firms were Westpac, the Commonwealth Bank, NAB, BHP and ANZ. Today, they are Westpac, the Commonwealth Bank, NAB, BHP and CSL. A stock-trading Rip Van Winkle who went to sleep in the 1980s and woke up now would be amazed by the US market but not at all startled by the Australian market.

It gets worse if we go all the way back to 1917.[23] None of America's top ten companies then are still in the top ten today. But of Australia's top ten companies at the end of World War I, five still make the list today. Although some have changed their names, Westpac, ANZ, NAB, BHP and Wesfarmers have enjoyed more than a century at the top of the Australian sharemarket. They were our top companies when Don Bradman was in primary school, and they're still there today.

The average Australian company is considerably older than firms in other countries. Weighted by market capitalisation, the average listed company in Australia today is 105 years old, compared with ninety-five in Britain, eighty-two in the United States and seventy-seven in Japan. Just 234 years after European settlement, there is something peculiar about the fact that Australia's typical listed firm is more than a century old. Australians can be proud of our venerable companies, but the situation is akin to Little Athletics collapsing while the Masters Games boom. It doesn't bode well for the future.

Boosting productivity requires new answers. For example, maybe we need to revamp knowledge work. In companies large and small, work has become what technology writer Cal Newport calls 'constant multitasking craziness'.[24] The typical office worker checks their email every six minutes, and people are often distracted by what they find. Emails frequently leave issues partially resolved, leading to a back-and-forth exchange that cuts across other tasks. The solution, according to Newport, is to implement top-down reforms that allow employees to better deploy their 'attention capital'. One promising example is extreme programming, a style of work in which computer coders collaborate in pairs to solve hard problems, with no expectation of checking email or web surfing. This kind of work is so focused that those who are new to it often feel 'zapped' when they clock off at 5 p.m.

Organisations that experiment with ways of encouraging 'deep work' (focusing on a task without distraction) may well be the first to experience large improvements in productivity. But in a sense, all they will be doing is replicating the way in which an effective sporting team operates. You don't see first-grade cricketers checking email while they're fielding in the slips—they have one job and they're totally focused on it.

At last year's Tokyo Olympics, Australia was ranked sixth on the medal tally. But we don't rank anywhere near that high for economic innovation. New athletes are shaking up sports from surfing to CrossFit, BMX to rowing. But while our world champions are young and dynamic, Australia's largest companies are centenarians. Mobility across jobs and regions is down, while productivity and wage growth have slowed. The economy needs to be more dynamic, creating more startups, finding entrepreneurial talent in unexpected places, and ensuring that knowledge workers can engage in deep work. And to produce a fitter economy, we need to draw on something beloved by all true sportspeople: a dose of healthy competition.

GOOD RULES MAKE A GOOD GAME

Football has ancient origins. In ancient China, players stood in a circle and tried to keep a ball in the air. Native Americans, Indigenous Australians and Māoris played games that involved teams trying to score by moving a ball forward. The modern game had its genesis in the nineteenth century, when several English schools formalised the rules of football. This led to some unusual regulations. Harrow Football used a ball that resembled a heavy pork pie, and it allowed players to tackle opponents who didn't possess the ball and to catch the ball in their hands on the full. Eton Football was played along a wall and awarded extra points for a 'rouge', in which the ball deflects off a defender on the way to the goal. The Rugby School game allowed 'hacking', basically kicking opposing players in the shins.

Written rules allowed the game to be played regularly in individual schools, but football could not take off as a sport until different teams agreed on how to play the game. By the mid-1800s, cricket's rules were settled, so contests between villages were common. But even although football required less equipment, it could not become a mass-participation sport while everyone played by different rules. In 1863, representatives of the football-playing schools drew up the Football Association laws, leading to the game that in Australia we have long called soccer—although it is increasingly, and in step with international usage, becoming known as 'football'. Eight years later, the Rugby Football Union was formed.

With the rules settled, both kinds of football quickly took off, expanding beyond its schoolboy roots and attracting tens of thousands of spectators. The first Rugby international game took place between Scotland and England in 1871. Soccer has been an Olympic sport since 1900, and the formation in 1904 of the Fédération Internationale de Football Association, or FIFA, was critical to ensuring the success of 'the world game'. By sorting out the rules, this football code got the jump on the other variations when it came to expanding across the globe. In terms of fans and players, it is the world's most popular sport.[25]

Settling the rules is fundamental to expanding the game. In Australia, Ireland and the United States, football codes took ideas from the English school rules, adapting them to create Aussie Rules, Gaelic football and American football (gridiron). The origin of American football terms such as 'quarterback' and 'downs', for example, can be traced back to older English games. Each game evolved, with Aussie Rules requiring players to bounce the ball and installing behind posts. According to one account, the rules of Australian football emerged because the game was played on hard paddocks, where the risk of injury was higher than on softer English fields.[26]

Football codes continue to adapt their rules to strike the right balance between safety and entertainment, and between offensive and defensive play. In 1905, a year in which eighteen American footballers died while playing the game, president Theodore Roosevelt held a summit at the White House, leading to reforms which made the game safer. Today, in Aussie Rules, technology is used to supplement the work of the referees, but the demands of the enormous television audience have also led to changes that reduce stoppage time. The objective is a game that is fast, fair and fun.

Healthy competition is also what economists want for the economy.[27] Competition keeps prices low and encourages companies to innovate. If consumers can choose between suppliers, they are less likely to be gouged on price. If employees can choose where to work, they are more likely to earn a decent wage and to be treated with decency. Competition also boosts innovation, leading to better and safer products. There's even some evidence that robust competition can reduce discrimination.[28] In the US banking system during the 1970s and 1980s, greater competition led to women earning higher wages.[29] When corporate margins are thin, it's harder for bigoted bosses to simply hire their buddies. Similarly, more competitive sporting codes tend to have less racial discrimination. As Major League Baseball became more competitive, racial pay gaps narrowed.[30] Competitive pressure encourages companies to hire the best people.

Ideally, if the rules of a sport are fair, and every athlete gets a chance to train, then vigorous competition becomes a force for egalitarianism. When Kenyan runners began dominating the marathon, they didn't do it because they were richer or had better shoes. Kenyan athletes benefited from dynamic competition and increasing prize pools, which allowed them to show the world what their genes and training could produce. Success in distance running has helped reduce poverty in Kenya, a country where the average income is just US$5 per day. The World Marathon Majors have created an annual global contest, and runners from Kenya's Rift Valley have won a remarkable share of the prizes.

Alas, many Australian industries are uncompetitive. When it comes to department stores, newspapers, banking, health insurance, supermarkets, domestic airlines, internet service providers, baby food and beer, the four biggest companies comprise more than four-fifths of the market.[31] In fact, it's hard to come up with examples of Australian industries that are *not* dominated by a couple of behemoths.

A lack of competition most hurts the poor. If you don't have a car, you can't drive to a cheap supermarket. If you don't have a good internet connection, you can't hop online to get a better deal. Poorer Australians are less likely to have the cash on hand to take advantage of bulk discounts, and they're more likely to have to rely on high-cost borrowing through payday loans and credit cards with excessive interest rates. To disadvantaged Australians, competitive markets aren't a luxury—they're a necessity. The referee should be especially looking out for the most vulnerable players on the field.

Monopoly power transfers resources from consumers to shareholders. Because shareholding is more skewed than consumption, that worsens inequality. Among the super-rich, one-quarter made their money by dominating an uncompetitive industry.[32] The worst arrangements come when market power goes hand in hand with disproportionate political influence. That's like a football team that wins the premiership, then uses its profits to buy board seats on the sport's governing body so it can rig the rules in its favour.

Companies with fewer competitors sometimes abuse their customers' trust. Shoe giant Reebok copped a US$350 000 fine for falsely claiming that its shoes would give walkers more muscular buttocks than traditional walking shoes. Activewear company Lorna Jane was fined $5 million for claiming its clothes stopped the spread of COVID, a statement the judge in the case called 'exploitative, predatory, and potentially dangerous'. Because Reebok and Lorna Jane are big brands, customers are more likely to fall for their falsehoods. Without a sharp-eyed referee, there's little to stop foul play.

From time to time, special interest groups claim that Australia must let certain companies dominate the local market so they can grow big enough to take on the world. This is the so-called 'national champions' argument. But just as on the athletics field, it turns out that wrapping your best in cotton wool isn't the way to attain Olympic gold. Uncompetitive markets tend to be less innovative and have fewer startups. If you can't win fairly at home, you don't have much hope overseas.

Diversity matters. If you're an Aussie Rules fan, you can choose between eighteen clubs. If you're a Super Netball fan, there are eight teams to choose from. But there aren't many sectors of the economy with eight serious competitors, let alone eighteen. Indeed, while sporting codes are fostering new teams such as the Greater Western Sydney Giants and the Tasmania JackJumpers, the trend in business is towards mergers. Over the past thirty years, the number of corporate mergers has grown by a factor of six, and the value of mergers has grown by a factor of eleven.[33] This has led to a substantial increase in market concentration in supermarkets, banking, airlines, meat processing, bottled drinks, telecommunications and a range of other important industries.[34] If sports teams had been buying out their rivals at the same rate, we'd all be barracking for the same few teams. According to Rod Sims, at the time head of the Australian Competition and Consumer Commission, increasing market power means that consumers pay more, farmers earn less, and small businesses are constrained.[35]

Collusion in some Australian industries is reminiscent of a story that screenwriter David Williamson tells about making the movie *Phar Lap*:

> We had to replicate the exact winning order of the horses in the 1930 Melbourne Cup, which Phar Lap won, and I remember asking some of our jockeys whether it was possible to do this. They looked at each other and burst out laughing. Sure enough, the horses crossed the winning line in perfect order and every one of the jockeys looked as if he was trying his heart out.[36]

Big tech poses big challenges. Uber owns no cars. Airbnb owns no hotels. Netflix has no stores. Yet they have transformed the taxi, accommodation and video industries. Apple, Google and Facebook have powerful monopolies over iPhone apps, internet searches and social media ads. These organisations are less like a sporting team and more like the people who run the entire competition.

Empowering the referees makes the game fairer. In tennis, the Hawk-Eye system tells umpires whether a ball was in or out. In cricket, infrared cameras assist umpires in determining if the ball has struck the bat or pad. Video referees are common in most football codes. Likewise, the competition watchdog needs the right powers and resources to tackle monopolies. When the agency says that it can't stop a bad merger, the rest of us should sit up and listen.[37]

In deterring bad behaviour, our laws are only as power-ful as the penalties courts can impose. Over the course of his fifteen-year career, tennis player John McEnroe was fined fourteen times for bad behaviour, earning him the moniker 'Superbrat'. The fines totalled US$69 500, or around 0.5 per cent of the US$12.5 million in prize money that McEnroe earned as a player.[38] Little wonder that he kept swearing at umpires until he retired. Similarly, fining a multibillion-dollar company a few million dollars is unlikely to deter it from future misbehaviour.

In a competitive market, our big banks shouldn't be among the most profitable in the world. There shouldn't be a 'cheap day' to buy petrol. Consumers shouldn't have just two companies to choose from. Getting competition right isn't just about creating a stronger economy—it's also fundamental to forging a fairer society. Just as settling the rules of football was necessary to take it from a game played in a few English private schools to a set of games played around the world, the rules of the market are vital to expanding prosperity for all.

PAY THE PLAYERS PROPERLY

In 1905, the All Blacks toured Britain, the first Rugby Union side from either Australia or New Zealand to do so. Eight days after arriving by ship, the team played its first game against Durham, the English club championship runners-up and hot favourites. The All Blacks won 55 to 4, a result that was such a surprise that one newspaper incorrectly reported it as Durham 55, New Zealand 4. The misreporting wouldn't last long. Over the remainder of the tour, the All Blacks scored sixteen times as many points as they conceded. They played thirty-five matches, winning all but one. The New Zealanders were fitter than their British opponents (they were used to playing 45-minute halves, while the British played for 35 minutes), better organised (each player in the scrum had a defined position, while their British opponents decided positions as the players packed down) and innovative (the All Blacks had two five-eighths). So complete was the victory of the touring side that *Punch* magazine illustrated the rout with a cover drawing of a baby cub beating a lion. Yet, because Rugby was an amateur game, the players were given just 3 shillings a day to cover their expenses. The conquering cubs earned no salary.

Responding to criticism of Rugby Union's failure to pay its players, one English official snobbishly noted that 'if the working man cannot afford to play, he must do as other people have to do who want things they cannot afford—do without'.[39] Working men protested that this might be fine for a gentleman in possession of a family fortune, but it didn't help a labourer whose Rugby injury prevented him from earning a living the following week.

In Australia, a similar dispute played out. In 1907, Sydney Rugby Union player Alec Burdon injured his shoulder in a game. A barber, Burdon was unable to work and had to pay his own medical expenses. The message from officials was clear: if a working man couldn't cover his costs, he had no right to play. Fed up, a group of players met at the sports shop of legendary cricketer Victor Trumper, where they agreed to start a breakaway 'Rugby League'. The New South Wales Rugby Union expelled the players, who included HH 'Dally' Messenger, one of the greatest players of all time.[40]

The occupations of the twenty-two breakaway players are indicative. They included four labourers, two painters, a storeman, a waterside worker, a cleaner, a boilermaker and a fishmonger.[41] The officials in what would be called the New South Wales Rugby Football League included Henry Clement Hoyle, who had been fired by the railways for organising workers and would later serve in a Labor Cabinet. The first full-time secretary of the new league was Ted Larkin, who went on to win the state seat of Willoughby as a Labor member before tragically being killed in action on the first day of the Gallipoli campaign. HV 'Doc' Evatt, who would go on to lead the federal Labor Party, was one of the founders of Sydney University's Rugby League club.[42] When he first ran for Balmain, Evatt advertised in the game's official journal that he was 'the rugby league candidate'. League soon displaced Rugby Union in NSW and Queensland.

Rugby's great split illustrates a factor that was fundamental to the development of sport in general: enforced amateurism slowed the growth of team games. When the players didn't get a share of the gate takings, working-class athletes had less incentive to join the game. By contrast, football (soccer) decided relatively early on that it was comfortable with player payments—a key reason for its rapid rise.

Athletes have often had to fight to get their fair share. In 1970, the Victorian Football League Players' Association was formed after two Collingwood players, Des Tuddenham and Len Thompson, went on strike for three weeks to demand an increase in match payments.[43] In some sports, players' unions—generally called players' associations—have formed to campaign for better pay and conditions, while in others, norms have steadily evolved. Australia's greatest-ever marathon runner, Rob de Castella, told me that in the 1980s, Athletics Australia insisted on taking a share of the money he was paid by his shoe sponsor, on the grounds that Deek was an amateur. Thankfully, today's amateur runners no longer have to hand off a portion of their sponsorship fees.

We may not all be sports stars, but the issues they face are similar to those that crop up in workplaces across the nation. The Australian soccer players who refused to play a 1925 match for 10 shillings each were aggrieved by the fact that the previous game's gate takings had amounted to £4303. They didn't think it was fair that the entire team got paid less than £6.

Five years ago, Margaret Peacock and her fellow workers also went on strike at the nation's largest envelope-manufacturing plant.[44] Peacock worked at Australian Paper in the Melbourne suburb of Preston, where she earned $21 an hour. The workers' decision to strike was taken after their union, the Australian Manufacturing

Workers' Union, had gone to the Fair Work Commission three times. They were asking for a pay rise of 2.5 per cent a year over three years, but the company was offering a deal that averaged 1.6 per cent. Put another way, after inflation, Peacock and her fellow workers were asking for the tiniest of increases in their real wages, while their employer was offering them a real wage cut. After an eight-week strike, Australian Paper agreed to the workers' pay claim. Peacock estimated that the strike cost her and her husband, who also worked at the plant, around $7000 in lost earnings.

Lately, real wage growth has made snail-racing look like an action sport. For the first decade of the 2000s, it averaged around 1 per cent a year. Since 2012, real wages have barely budged. This shows up in the share of national income going to workers in the form of wages, salaries and superannuation benefits.[45] In mid-2020, the labour share of national income dropped below half for the first time since 1959.[46] The share of income going to workers was at its lowest level in six decades, while the profit share was at a record high.

Unscrupulous employers can be especially tempted to mistreat workers when the situation is temporary. A few years ago, Irish backpacker Aoife Cullen and her boyfriend picked up jobs in a pub in outback New South Wales.[47] Every week, they each worked at least seventy hours, yet they were paid just $350 plus accommodation and meals. They had hoped to get their visas extended by doing regional work, but improper documentation of their wages meant that their visa applications were denied, and the pair were forced to leave the country. 'It's just one of them things that, like, honestly, I will never get over in my life,' said Cullen. When COVID caused the supply of international students and working holidaymakers to evaporate, many employers couldn't persuade locals to fill the jobs. A common story concerned the 'lazy Australians' who weren't willing to roll up their sleeves and do a hard day's work. But it's also hard to dupe locals into doing jobs that don't pay properly.

For many Australians, work has become more precarious. Unlike sporting teams, which directly employ their players, many workers are now employed by labour hire firms. In sectors such as manufacturing and construction, more than a tenth of the workforce is employed through companies such as Workfast, Hays and Agri Labour Australia. Five per cent of employees are labour hire workers, compared with less than 1 per cent in the early 1990s.[48] Employers like labour hire because it's easier to upsize or downsize, but many employees have come to hate it because of the havoc it wreaks on their lives. Meanwhile, in the gig economy, companies such as Uber Eats, Deliveroo and Amazon Flex do not directly employ their workers either. As a result, many gig workers earn less than the minimum wage. When, in a two-month period in 2020, five delivery drivers died, none of their families received workers' compensation.[49] Hundreds of thousands of people work in the fast-growing gig economy, yet their 'boss' is an app and they have few rights.

Software has made work more precarious. A company that produces scheduling software boasts that its system can 'predict business and labour demand down to 15-minute increments', using historical sales data, competitors' activity and even weather patterns to 'keep labour costs under control'.[50] Almost a million Australians have a second job, but changeable work schedules can make it tough to keep two employers happy. Fluctuating incomes can cause a crisis for anyone trying to pay regular bills. Ironically, at a time when governments are telling employees that they need to re-skill, some face work schedules that are too unpredictable to allow them to sign up for regular training classes.

As we've seen, a lack of competition hurts consumers. Suppose your favourite sporting competition consisted only of the best two teams. Those teams might inflate ticket prices, knowing that they control access to the only game in town. Fans would either miss out on a seat or pay extortionate prices to attend. And a two-team tournament would hurt players, too. With plenty of teams in the comp, players are likely to find one that values their talents and pays them fairly. If they quarrel with the coach, they can switch to another club. However, with just a couple of teams to choose from, athletes would be stuck. They would be more likely to be underpaid, exploited or mistreated. Players, like fans, benefit from choice—what holds for consumers goes for workers too.

Big Australian companies have used a variety of clever tricks to put the squeeze on workers. Some put clauses in their employment contracts that prevent workers from readily switching to a competitor—if an employee wants to quit and work at another company in the same industry, they may have to wait for months, sometimes years, between the two jobs. This means less mobility and lower wages. These rules stifle startups as well, which means society gets less innovation. In other sectors, the restrictions apply to employers. Several big franchise chains, including McDonald's, Domino's and Bakers Delight, require operators to promise that they won't poach workers from other outlets.

Aussie Rules provides an example of how improving worker mobility can create a better outcome. At the end of 2012, 'free agency' reforms made it easier for AFL players to change clubs. Those footballers who switched tended to play better at their new club. In the 2021 AFL grand final between the Demons and the Bulldogs, one-quarter of the players had come to their team from a different side. Among them was forward Mitch Hannan, who had just switched from the Demons (the eventual premiers) to the Bulldogs.[51]

Mobility is good, but sticking together is even more important. Unions were formed when workers recognised that they could get a better deal by acting collectively. Sick leave, annual leave, parental leave, the eight-hour day, long-service leave and superannuation all have their origins not in the generosity of employers but in the campaigns of unions. Unions make workplaces safer and increase wages.[52] Yet they aren't as strong as they once were. Just one in seven workers is now in a union, down from half in the early 1980s. With a higher union-isation rate, people would earn more and suffer fewer workplace accidents.

A measure of what unions can deliver is highlighted by the case of the powerful Rugby League Players Association. In 2017, the association struck a deal that delivered the biggest pay rise in League history. Those who gained most were players on the minimum wage, which rose from $80 000 to $100 000—a 25 per cent increase. The pay deal saw players receive nearly one-third of game-day revenue, ensuring they benefited from successful games. A new fund was also set up to support players who had to retire early because of injury.

Rugby League hasn't suffered from raising its minimum wage, and nor will the economy if we pay entry-level workers a decent salary. Short-sighted businesses want low-paid workers and high-paid customers. Far-sighted businesses recognise that workers and customers are the same people. If you want to boost consumer spending, putting money into the hands of the lowest-paid workers is the best strategy.

When those Rugby players met in Victor Trumper's shop in 1907, they simply wanted a reasonable share of the gate takings. In creating Rugby League, they established a code that could be played by ordinary working people, those without family money. The players were inspired by fairness, not greed. Since then, League fans have been able to enjoy a game whose origins lay in a demand for good wages. Because, in the end, ensuring workers get their fair share is the decent thing to do. And don't we all care about decency?

BE KIND

On a mild Melbourne afternoon in 1956, a pack of runners set out on a four-lap race to determine Australia's fastest miler.[53] With a lap and a half to go, one of the runners clipped the heel of Ron Clarke, who fell to the track. Right behind him was John Landy, whose foot hit Clarke's shoulder. He stopped and turned to ask if Clarke was okay. By the time Clarke had replied, 'Yes, yes, go, go, run!', Landy had fallen 35 metres behind the rest of the pack. To the delight of the 25 000 fans packed into Olympic Park Stadium, he not only caught the other runners but went on to win by 10 metres.

The moment when Landy stopped to check on Clarke has been called 'the ultimate act of sportsmanship'. It is now immortalised by a statue at Olympic Park, near the former site of the now-demolished stadium. The image is reminiscent of the trophy given to NRL premiers, which depicts opposing captains Norm Provan and Arthur Summons embracing after the muddy 1963 grand final. That's right: the ultimate trophy in one of our roughest games shows two opponents hugging. Kindness even extends to boxing, as when in Tokyo last year, Harry Garside won Australia's first Olympic medal in the sport in a generation, then held open the ropes to let his opponent exit the ring first.

Australian cricketers have produced some of the best and worst moments of sportsmanship. An example of the former occurred just after the end of World War II, when a visiting English side was touring Queensland.[54] After the Australians had scored 600 runs in the first two days, an overnight tropical storm made the pitch all but unplayable for the tourists. English batsman Bill Edrich then faced Australian fast bowler Keith Miller, both of whom had flown repeated sorties over Germany during the war. When the ball kept hitting Edrich, Miller began to bowl more slowly. Edrich was a mate, thought Miller, and the Australians were going to win the match anyway. Even when captain Don Bradman asked him to bowl faster, Miller refused to risk injuring a man who had been awarded the Distinguished Flying Cross for his bravery.

In recent decades, Australian cricketers have made headlines for ball tampering, sledging and sexting. But such sour moments are the exception. The true spirit of cricket is embodied in the game that the Australian soldiers played in Gallipoli in 1915, two days before the evacuation. They played on Shell Green, which got its name because it was under constant Turkish artillery fire. As the shells whistled by, some players pretended to field them, laughing to show their lack of concern.[55] The spirit of cricket was also epitomised in an Australia–England game in the Japanese prisoner-of-war camp at Changi, Singapore in 1942, where men living on starvation rations played a series of matches using barracks and barbed wire as boundary fences. Amid beri-beri, dysentery and hunger, the players indulged the dream of playing for their country. England won all three games—partly because of the batting of Geoff Edrich, brother of the aforementioned Bill.[56]

We prize honour and decency in our sports stars because they are the kinds of values we want to see in our society. Too often, however, our economy fails to extend the kind of respect and dignity to working people that mark a decent society. I remember once hearing the story of a man who had been cleaning a school for over a decade. He had his own set of keys to the buildings, so he could do his work and then lock up the facilities. One day the cleaner was told that the school's management had determined it was too much of a risk for him to hold on to the keys. From then on, he would need to pick them up and drop them off at the cleaning company's office. The cleaner was crestfallen at the message implied by the decision: he could not be trusted.

A power imbalance in the workplace shapes the way in which employees are treated. A 2017 survey of retail and fast-food workers found that 85 per cent had been abused at work.[57] One said: 'I have had customers throw products at me [over] simple things such as a product is out of stock. I've had my face spat on, [been] slapped across the face and had one person … swing to punch me and miss (I dodged it).'

Another cruel feature of the modern labour market is unpredictable shifts. For many casual workers, this makes it hard to plan a visit to a dentist, tricky to organise child care, and difficult to be a reliable member of the local netball team. A US study of retail and fast-food workers found that one in three typically received less than a week's notice of their shifts, one in seven had a shift cancelled on them in the last month, and half had to work 'clopening' shifts (closing the store one day and opening it the next).[58] Workers with less predictable schedules were more likely to experience psychological distress and poor sleep quality, and less likely to say that they were happy with their lives.

One way to curb the growth in unsociable working hours is through penalty rates—pay loadings for working on nights, weekends or public holidays. From an economic standpoint, weekends exist for a simple reason: to solve the leisure coordination problem. Suppose two people want to meet up in a park one morning to kick a football around. In a world without weekends, both would have to coordinate their schedules with their employers. But in a world with weekends, they can simply get together on a Saturday or Sunday. Without weekends, adults would play less sport, parents would struggle to take their children to games, and the crowds watching major sporting events would be diminished. Penalty rates defend nights, weekends and public holidays. By requiring workers to be paid more for working at those times, they help safeguard a sense of community around families eating dinner together, neighbourhood groups scheduling evening meetings, and religious bodies holding weekend services. Penalty rates bolster a decent society in which people do not have to choose between earning and socialising.

When eating out on a public holiday, I've never objected to paying a menu surcharge to cover the penalty rates. For my family to enjoy a restaurant meal, someone else must miss out on precious holiday time with their family and friends. If you're at a café on Easter Monday, the person serving your table isn't able to experience the leisure time that most people take for granted on that long weekend.[59]

Leisure isn't just about weekends. Over the past century, campaigns for shorter working days and more annual leave have significantly reduced the number of hours worked by the typical employee.[60] But we could still argue that attempts to reduce working hours have fallen short. In 1930, John Maynard Keynes penned 'Economic Possibilities for Our Grandchildren', an essay which predicted that, by 2030, the global economy would expand eightfold, and average working hours would fall to three hours a day.[61] Economic growth has already outstripped Keynes's predictions, but most employees work far more than three hours a day. Indeed, in Australia, full-timers work longer hours than in most advanced nations.[62]

The last major working hours campaign was that for four weeks' annual leave, which succeeded nationally in 1974. In the half-century since, there has not been a serious push to reduce Australian working hours. This is despite the fact that nations such as France, Austria, Spain and Sweden offer their employees five weeks of annual leave. There is evidence that Australians would like more annual leave. In a survey conducted in the early 2000s, most respondents said they would prefer two additional weeks to the same proportionate increase in wages (4 per cent).[63]

Another area that needs reform is sick leave. When COVID-19 struck, it highlighted the fact that one-quarter of workers were not entitled to sick leave. If these workers became a close contact, they often had to choose between missing a pay packet or risking infecting others. Somehow, society had come to accept that there was a class of workers who had to suffer economically when they fell ill. It reminded me of the way contact sports like Rugby League once saw head injuries as an inevitable part of the game. Today, a recognition of the dangers of such trauma has led to the greater use of head-protection gear, recognition of the risks of concussions, and research on retired players to monitor long-term risks. The old approach to head injuries was not only dangerous, it lacked decency.

Decency also needs to be restored to manual jobs in general. On shows such as *The Simpsons*, *Home Improvement* and *All in the Family*, working-class dads are depicted as bumbling and inept.[64] This snobbery can make blue-collar workers feel that their work is somehow second-rate. Except on the sporting field, ours is a society where people are increasingly rewarded for brains rather than brawn.

Honouring the dignity of work, an idea put forward by Harvard philosopher Michael Sandel and British parliamentarian Jon Cruddas, is one solution to this problem.[65] It recognises that, for most of us, our identity is determined by our status as producers, not consumers. And it calls for a society that celebrates jobs for what they contribute to the common good, not just for what they pay. As Martin Luther King put it, 'the person who picks up our garbage is in the final analysis as significant as the physician, for if he doesn't do his job, diseases are rampant. All labour has dignity'.[66] We may not be John Landy or Keith Miller, but a labour market inspired by their kindness is one that works for all.

EVERYONE DESERVES A GREAT COACH

Dawn Fraser was encouraged to swim when, at ten years of age, she realised that swimming eased her asthma.[67] Simone Biles was introduced to gymnastics at age six, after spending her early years in foster care. Scottish tennis player Andy Murray survived the Dunblane school massacre by hiding under a desk. Clara Hughes, the only person to have won multiple medals at the Summer and Winter Olympics, spent her early teens drinking, smoking and taking hard drugs.[68] The coaches of Fraser, Biles, Murray and Hughes focused on their talents, not their trauma. Coaches must nurture their athletes while pushing them to go further.

Alisa Camplin recalls a running coach who set her the task of doing ten 400-metre sprints on a hot afternoon when she was thirteen years old.[69] After the session, he asked her how the last two repetitions had gone. 'Brutal', replied Camplin. What she didn't realise was that the coach had been watching her session. 'I know you only did eight,' he said. 'You'll never amount to anything if you cheat yourself'. Camplin felt humiliated, but the exchange 'influenced every choice and action I've made over the course of my life'. At age nineteen, she switched from running to ski jumping, despite never having seen snow. Over the next eight years, Camplin would break ribs, ankles and her collarbone, tear her knee ligaments, and experience multiple concussions. At the 2002 Salt Lake City Winter Olympics, she won gold. Great coaches and sports psychologists were essential to her success.

One of Australia's most remarkable coaches was Percy Cerutty, whose training camp at Portsea in Victoria combined motivational lectures, year-round swimming, a strict diet and running up dunes. His greatest runner, Herb Elliott, once reflected: 'I have known a lot of pain, and so you would dread the training sessions. But during them you were totally focused on the challenge of not giving in to yourself and, at the end … the satisfaction sort of outweighed the pain.'[70] At the 1960 Rome Olympics, Elliott won the 1500 metres by almost 20 metres. Reporters said he made the other runners look like schoolboys.

Two of Australia's greatest Indigenous athletes, Evonne Goolagong Cawley and Cathy Freeman, were spotted by talent scouts at a young age. Goolagong grew up in Barellan, which had its share of prejudiced people, but she caught a break when a tennis player saw her peering through the court fence and invited her in for a hit. A few years later, Vic Edwards, the manager of a Sydney tennis school, heard about Goolagong's talent and persuaded her to move to Sydney, where she lived with Edwards and his family as he became her coach and manager.

Raised in regional Queensland, Cathy Freeman won a scholarship to attend Fairholme Presbyterian Girls' College in Toowoomba, and then to go to Kooralbyn International School in the Gold Coast hinterland. At Kooralbyn, she trained under Mike Danila, a Romanian immigrant who increased the intensity of her training. As Freeman recalls, 'He was always harder on me. Some of the others had days off, but I wasn't allowed to miss training.'[71] Contemplating the stories of Goolagong and Freeman, we can only imagine how many more Indigenous athletes might have become world champions if they had the right coaches.

My own coaches have shaped much more than sport. As a child, my race-walking coach Yvonne Melene took me from being one of the most unfit kids in my primary school to winning a gold teams medal at the Australian high school championships. Even on the rainiest night, I knew Melene would be at training, so there was no excuse for staying home. As an adult, I've been lucky to run marathons under the tutelage of Dick Telford, piggybacking on the training sessions he sets for his elite runners—from long runs to painful track sessions. Running as a supporter of Rob de Castella's Indigenous Marathon Foundation, I've internalised Deek aphorisms such as 'The marathon deserves respect' and 'Hills make you strong'. While I was preparing for an Ironman triathlon, Ben Gathercole turned my clumsy freestyle into something more closely resembling a smooth stroke, and helped me figure out how to squeeze training between work and family commitments. I'm a stronger athlete, and a better person, because of their coaching.

Just as remarkable coaches help sportspeople to achieve physical feats, the best educators enable their students to fulfil their intellectual potential. Higher levels of schooling reduce the chances that people will go on to commit a crime, by improving their self-control and encouraging long-term thinking.[72] Education also makes for a more engaged citizenry—more likely to participate in civic activities, join a political party, and run for office. Education even helps you breathe a little better, as those with more schooling are more likely to engage in physical activity, less likely to smoke, and more likely to say that they are in good health.

And that's before we get to the biggest benefit of education: its impact on earnings. Estimates vary, but one rule of thumb is that, across high school and university, an additional year of education boosts lifetime earnings by at least 10 per cent.[73] This means that completing a degree is worth around $600 000 to the typical Australian woman, and $800 000 to the typical Australian man.[74]

Across the nation, hundreds of thousands of talented educators are doing their best. Yet, as a whole, the Australian education system is not living up to its potential. Just look at the Programme for International Student Assessment (PISA) tests run by the Organisation for Economic Cooperation and Development (OECD). These tests are designed to go beyond rote learning to assess students' critical thinking and problem-solving skills—vital talents in a digital age. Since 2000, OECD boffins have come to Australia every few years to test the country's teens. Each time, on each test, performance has declined. The drop in reading equates to around three-quarters of a year of schooling. The drop in maths is equivalent to more than one year of schooling. The drop in science corresponds to nearly one year of schooling.[75] In other words, a year 8 student educated at the turn of the millennium would do almost as well as a year 9 student educated today.

Just imagine the shock if the nation's sporting teams were performing this poorly. Imagine if the skill of today's first-grade teams had slumped to the level of reserve-grade teams a few decades ago. Suppose our swimmers were getting slower, posting times that were seconds off the pace of previous winners. Imagine if this generation's Aussie Rules players couldn't kick as far, its netballers were less likely to make their shots, and its powerlifters couldn't lift as much weight. As a nation, we'd know something was seriously amiss.

What's going wrong? One possibility is a decline in teacher quality. My own research suggests that the most effective tenth of teachers produce twice the test score gains as the least effective tenth of teachers.[76] In other words, the most effective teachers can do in a single day what the least effective teachers do in two days. Yet the academic aptitude of new teachers has declined over recent decades, which might explain why Australia's PISA scores have gone backwards.[77] Measured in terms of the earnings boost for their students, talented teachers are literally worth their weight in gold.[78] Making teacher quality the central focus of schools policy would also help address other challenges. With a first-rate teaching workforce, debates around the frequency of testing and the flexibility of the curriculum become less important. Talented educators will succeed in many different settings, adapting their approach to serve the needs of the students.

Beyond secondary school, vocational training is falling short of its potential. Vocational education completion numbers rose steadily from the mid-1990s through the early 2010s, peaking in 2013.[79] Since then, the numbers have collapsed. On a per-person basis, the share of people completing an apprenticeship or traineeship in 2020 was less than one-third of what it had been in 2013. Dropout rates are massive: for every five people who start a vocational qualification, just two finish it.[80]

In the university sector, the biggest problem is access. Attendance rates increased markedly when Australia adopted a demand-driven system in 2012. It meant that places were set based on what students wanted to study, rather than being micromanaged by the education department. In less than a decade, the share of nineteen-year-olds at university rose from three in ten to four in ten.[81] Among the fastest-growing disciplines were health, natural sciences and information technology.[82] The new students were disproportionately from needy backgrounds, with the share of students from disadvantaged neighbourhoods increasing significantly. The end of the demand-driven system in 2017 caused tertiary attendance to stall. Just as those who benefited from the shift to that arrangement were disproportionately from disadvantaged backgrounds, so too the cessation of the demand-driven system has disproportionately denied opportunities to low-income students.

As well as expanding the number of university places, universities can do a better job of talent scouting—identifying promising students from disadvantaged backgrounds.[83] Universities might learn from the way that sports are using data and technology to cast the talent net as wide as possible. In 2016, Zwift, an online cycling and running game, launched its Zwift Academy, inviting any cyclist to compete against the world's best. Several winners secured contracts with professional cycling teams. Zwift is a reminder that cheap, high-quality, online training can massively improve access to education for less-conventional students.

As a runner, one of my favourite motivational lines is from the Greek poet Archilochus: 'We don't rise to the level of our expectations; we fall to the level of our training.' As a nation, our education system will be a fundamental determinant of whether we achieve our hopes and dreams. If we don't train right, we won't accomplish our goals.

When Australia failed to win a gold medal at the 1976 Montreal Olympics, it was seen as a national calamity. The Montreal debacle led to the creation of the Australian Institute of Sport, and a steady climb back up the medal rankings in subsequent Olympics. Australia's education crisis demands a full-court press to turn our game around.

PARTICIPATION MATTERS

In *Why We Swim*, Bonnie Tsui describes how the 'act of swimming can be one of healing, and health—a way to well-being. Swimming together can be a way to find community, through a team, a club, or a shared, beloved body of water'. She goes on to observe: 'Swimming is about the mind, too. To find rhythm in the water is to discover a new way of being in the water, through flow'.[84]

Over the two years he lived by Walden Pond, Henry David Thoreau started each day with a swim, calling it 'a religious exercise, and one of the best things which I did'.[85] For my own part, I love the simplicity of the activity—the meditative way in which an easy swim lets your mind wander, the intensity of a lung-busting sprint session, the crystalline beauty of an outdoor pool in the summer. And I enjoy the camaraderie of a swim squad— the encouragement of the coach, the cajoling of fellow swimmers, the banter in the showers afterwards.

Others love to run. In ancient times in Africa's Serengeti region, humans hunted animals by exhaustion-running—chasing their prey until the beast was too tired to go any further. Christopher McDougall argues that, for our species, running is inextricably connected to our evolution: 'You had to love running, or you wouldn't live to love anything else. And like everything else we love—everything we sentimentally call our "passions" and "desires"—it's really an encoded ancestral necessity. We were born to run; we were born because we run.'[86]

I've run a few dozen marathons, but my favourite was the Tokyo Marathon, where they moved us into the starting corrals almost an hour before the gun went off. To settle my nerves, I'd loaded onto my smartphone the ebook of Japanese novelist Haruki Murakami's memoir *What I Talk about When I Talk about Running*. Murakami discusses how he came to running in his thirties. He runs every day not because he wants to live longer, but because he wants to live life to the fullest. Novel writing, Murakami says, is an unhealthy activity. To deal with it, 'a person needs to be as healthy as possible', since 'an unhealthy soul requires a healthy body'.[87] Inspired by Murakami's musings on the pleasure of running, I literally whooped when the starting gun fired and ran my quickest-ever marathon, in a time of 2 hours and 42 minutes.

Cycling is equally exhilarating. Ever since the invention of the penny-farthing, cyclists have relished the joy of moving quickly under their own power. Frenchman Jean Bobet describes the exhilaration of a perfect ride as 'La Volupté': 'The voluptuous pleasure that cycling can give you is delicate, intimate and ephemeral. It arrives, it takes hold of you, sweeps you up and then leaves you again. It is for you alone. It is a combination of speed and ease, force and grace. It is pure happiness.'[88]

Occasionally, I'll join a bunch of riders who meet at 6 a.m. for an hour-long ride around Canberra. My favourite rides are in summer, when we shed the leggings and jackets and enjoy the warm air whipping by us. On one such morning, as we crested a hill to see the sun rising in front of us, the bloke on the bike next to me quipped, 'I wouldn't be dead for quids.'

Swimming, running and cycling are among my favourite sports, but there are hundreds of others to choose from. Sport helps us live longer and makes us think better. Exercising outdoors can connect us with nature, and working out with others can provide a sense of shared community. If exercise was a pill, it would be a wonder drug. We live in an era when waistlines are widening— as food is getting tastier and jobs are becoming more sedentary. That makes exercise more important than ever. When it comes to sport, participation matters.

While the Australian economy has created millions of jobs over recent decades, it has not delivered for everyone. Job loss has been most extensive among so-called 'routine' jobs, those involving repetitive work with limited human interaction.[89] Routine jobs have tended to pay middling wages: higher than manual jobs such as sales and cleaning, but lower than abstract jobs such as managers and professionals. Since the 1960s, routine jobs such as data entry, repetitive factory work and quality testing have shrunk. Meanwhile, the number of manual jobs in

Australia has increased, with strong demand for security guards, carers and manicurists. At the same time, the number of abstract jobs has grown, with increasing numbers of data analysts, financial dealers and web designers. As these average-pay occupations disappear, the people who do them are cascading down into lower-paid occupations. So there are growing numbers of security guards and baristas, but because these occupations don't require a great deal of training, the increase in demand for their services hasn't translated into an increase in their wages.

A solidly built man in his late fifties, 'Tom' is one of those who've been left behind by these changes. When I met him, he hadn't worked in more than two years. As a teenager, Tom told me, he couldn't wait to leave school. When he dropped out at the end of year 10, his teachers told his parents that he'd attained a fifth-grade literacy level. Even today, Tom leaves it to his wife to write things for him. He tried using a computer but said that it made him feel so frustrated that he nearly ended up throwing it off the desk.

It's not as though Tom doesn't have any skills. For years he worked as a delivery driver. 'I don't need a GPS', he told me when he dropped by my office for a chat. 'Just tell me where you need to go and I'll figure it out.' He says he's also pretty good at fixing cars, though he admits that he finds the new models trickier: 'Too many computers in them.' But there's bursitis in Tom's right shoulder, and he gets a pain on the left side of his chest. He also suffers from anxiety when he's faced with tight deadlines. In his last job, when his boss told him that everything had be to done under the pressure of a six-hour shift, he couldn't stay on. Tom doesn't mind working, but he hates strict timetables.

As we discuss what comes next, Tom talks about jobs in garbage disposal and asbestos removal. He'd be happy to be the lollipop person who manages a school crossing. But after years of knockbacks, he's tired of applying to employers who want someone younger and more energetic.

In recent decades, the Australian labour market has been reshaped by technology and globalisation. These twin forces can each have a similar impact. Suppose we create a machine that turned iron ore into televisions. If you dump a shipload of iron ore into the machine, it would churn out 2000 TVs. In fact, you could call this a 'trade machine', since it's exactly how trade works—exporting minerals and importing electronic goods. You can also think of the change in the terms of trade during the mining boom as being like a big technological improvement. By the peak of the boom, the trade machine turned a shipload of iron ore into 20 000 televisions.[90]

In general, technology tends to give the most to those who already get the most. Machines are particularly effective at taking the place of workers doing routine jobs. When I worked as a junior lawyer in the early 1990s, the law firm had a pool of typists whose job was to transcribe dictation. Once lawyers all had computers on their desks, the typists were gone. Law firms of that era also engaged paralegals to pore over thousands of pages of documents

relating to lawsuits, but with advances in artificial intel-
ligence and text recognition, such jobs are disappearing.
Technology has been great for law partners but lousy
for typists.

What do we do when work disappears? A popular
answer has been to accept the loss of work as inevitable.
In recent years, an odd coalition of Silicon Valley entrepreneurs and progressive activists have argued that,
rather than fighting to retain good jobs, we should adapt
to a world in which worklessness is increasingly normal.
Instead of focusing on job creation, they argue, everyone
should be provided with a universal basic income (UBI).

A UBI would cost a bomb, but its biggest flaw is that it
fails to acknowledge the role that work plays in a good life.
A fulfilling job provides a sense of meaning and dignity
that goes well beyond the pay packet. Research on job
loss and happiness followed a group of Australians over
time and found that life satisfaction dipped markedly
when people lost their jobs. Indeed, the drop in satisfaction went well beyond the loss of earnings. To restore the
happiness of an unemployed person, they would have to
receive $40 000 to $80 000 more than they were earning
in their job.[91] I noticed this in my conversation with Tom,
whose inability to find work had left him feeling pro-
foundly neglected by society. Doing the kind of work that
society honours provides satisfaction, not just a salary.

Work has become more sedentary, but you'd be hard-
pressed to find a health expert who thinks that the answer
is to do less exercise. Likewise, few economists think we

should give up on full employment in the face of technological innovation. Participation in the world of work, like participation in the world of exercise, is fundamentally important to maintaining quality of life. Throughout human history, we have worked and moved our bodies. Both physically and intellectually, activity is good for us.

Part of the answer is to meet technological change with a better-skilled workforce. One of the best predictors of whether someone has a job is their level of education. Among working-age adults with a university degree, eight out of ten have jobs. Of those adults who did not finish year 10, just four out of ten are working. Basically, someone with a university degree is twice as likely to be employed as someone who did not finish year 10.

In principle, anyone can retrain. But in practice, few adults relish the prospect of going back into the classroom. Governments can also create jobs for people who were formerly unemployed, which involves a bit of a mindshift. We're used to governments boldly announcing that a program employing ten people has 'created ten jobs'. Yet that is rarely the reality. Let's use a sports analogy. Suppose Australia decided to form an elite squad of ten runners, targeted at attempting to see how many people could break the 4-minute mile in a single event. It's unlikely that any of these runners were previously sedentary, so the impact on the total number of runners in Australia is likely to be nil. But if you persuade ten friends to join a 'Couch to 5k' program, the aim of which is to get participants to go from couch potato to running 5 kilometres within a few months, then you have increased the number of runners in the country—at least for as long as they stick with the program.

To create jobs, you need to start with people who don't have jobs. Targets for the employment of Indigenous Australians and people with disabilities can reduce joblessness, since both groups experience higher-than-average levels of unemployment. Programs such as Indigenous rangers, which is focused on land management and conservation, provide opportunities in regional and remote communities, and to people without formal qualifications. Local councils are the tier of government with the best track record of providing jobs to the unemployed, in areas such as maintaining sports ovals, staffing public libraries and building new footpaths.

By definition, government jobs involve the government paying 100 per cent of the wage. But there are also intriguing examples in which governments pay only part of the wage. In many other advanced nations, governments subsidise the wages of people with low earnings. For example, the United States Earned Income Tax Credit provides a single parent with two children a 40 per cent wage top-up if they earn less than US$15 000. The program creates a big incentive for such a person to take on a low-wage job, since a US$20 hourly wage effectively becomes a US$28 hourly wage after the subsidies are included. While a UBI discourages work, wage subsidies encourage it. For the lowest earners, the principle is simple: the more you work, the more wage subsidies the government pays you. And because the government is only paying a portion of the wage, it can assist more people than if it covered the entire wage bill.

When COVID-19 hit, wage subsidies were one of the most common ways in which advanced countries responded. Some made their existing schemes more generous, while other nations—including Australia, New Zealand and Canada—created entirely new programs. These schemes saved jobs, but the quality of their targeting varied enormously. For example, Australia's JobKeeper program was undoubtedly responsible for keeping people employed in sectors that experienced near-total shutdown, such as aviation. But over one-fifth of JobKeeper payments went to firms with rising turnover, bumping up the cost of the program. As a result, the average full-year cost of each job that was saved ended up at between \$140 000 and \$204 000: considerably higher than what most people earn.[92] Wage subsidies need to be better targeted if they are to do the most good.

Just as exercise is for everyone, participation in employment should be available to anyone. Full employment is not a relic of the past but a worthy goal in the modern age. Job-creation programs and wage subsidies, while making mid-career retraining affordable and accessible, will help ensure jobs for all.

WINNING WOMEN

Sarah 'Fanny' Durack learned to swim at Sydney's Coogee Baths during 'ladies hour'. When she was a teenager, her main rival was Wilhelmina 'Mina' Wylie, the daughter of the man who ran Wylie's Baths, also in Coogee. The two vied with one another in schoolgirl competitions, with Durack setting three world records. Yet, when the organisers of the 1912 Stockholm Olympics announced that women's swimming would be on the program for the first time, the all-male Australian selectors decided to send seven men and no women. Durack and Wylie were forced to ask the public for donations to pay their fares for the long boat journey to Sweden, each accompanied by a chaperone. In the first-ever women's Olympic swimming event, the 100 metres freestyle, Durack won gold and Wylie took silver. As one commentator noted, if Australia had sent two more women swimmers, they could surely have won the 4 × 100-metre relay.[93]

The story of women in sport is intertwined with the broader struggle for equality. The dictators Adolf Hitler and Benito Mussolini banned strenuous sport for women, absurdly suggesting that it interfered with their roles as wives and mothers. Conversely, pioneers of women's equality often began with sport. Vida Goldstein, an Australian suffragette of international repute, was the first president of the Victorian Ladies' Cricket Association.[94] Jessie Street, the most prominent Australian feminist of the postwar era, captained Sydney University's women's hockey team and was a founding member of the university's Women's Sports Association.

Women in sport have had to fight off plenty of detractors. Vigorous exercise was said to harm women's reproductive potential. Before the first Australian women's golf championship in 1894, a commentator wrote: 'Constitutionally and physically women are unfitted for golf … The first ladies' championship will be the last.'[95] This would be news today to successful women golfers such as Karrie Webb, who has won seven majors—more than Greg Norman. Similarly, we can only shake our heads at the *West Australian* editorial writer who in 1895 claimed that 'Ladies, however ingenious and versatile, are apparently not designed for football playing'.[96] If only the curmudgeonly scribe could have lived to see Tayla Harris kick, and the AFL Women's tournament drawing a television audience of over one million viewers.

Some extraordinarily tenacious athletes have helped the cause of gender equality. In 1967, Kathrine Switzer registered for the Boston Marathon under the name 'KV Switzer' and set out to be the first woman to run the 42-kilometre race. About 10 kilometres in, a race official grabbed her and attempted to remove her race bib, snarling 'Get the hell out of my race and give me those numbers!'[97] Other runners stood up for her and Switzer went on to complete the race. Today, women comprise 48 per cent of Boston Marathon runners.[98] It's a similar story at the Olympics. At the 1984 Los Angeles Olympics, there were twice as many men's events as women's events, and men made up three-quarters of the competitors.[99] By the 2021 Tokyo games, 49 per cent of the athletes were women, with several countries—including Australia, China and the United States—sending majority-female squads.[100]

The achievements of women in sport are sometimes thought to be impossible until they are realised. In 2015, Michelle Payne beat the world's best jockeys to win the Melbourne Cup. Diana Nyad is the only person to have swum from Cuba to the United States. Amanda Coker holds the record for the furthest distance cycled in a year. In these sports, the success of women has defined the frontiers of what is humanly possible.

Equal pay, however, has long been an issue in sport. When tennis player Billie Jean King won the US Open in 1972, her prize was $10 000, while the men's competition winner received $25 000. King refused to play the following year unless the prizes were equalised. The US Open yielded, but it took until 2007 for Wimbledon to provide equal prizes to men and women. While pay gaps remain large in traditionally male sports such as football and cricket, Australian hockey treats men and women equally. As former Hockey Australia chief executive Cam Vale summed it up, 'We treat our athletes as athletes. Whether you're a Kookaburra or a Hockeyroo, when it comes to the basic terms and principles in how we remunerate our athletes, it's exactly the same.'[101]

Many sports are still a long way from achieving gender parity. Still, the gender mix of the Australian Olympic squad stands in stark contrast to those who run Australian firms. Only 6 per cent of Australia's largest 300 companies have a female chief executive.[102] Fewer big companies are run by women than by men named John. Just 3 per cent of public sculptures honour real Australian women—fewer than the number that depict animals.[103] An analysis of 57 000 news media articles found that only 35 per cent were written by women journalists and just 31 per cent of the quotes were from women.[104] On this score, sport does especially poorly, with just 13 per cent of sport stories written by female journalists and only 16 per cent of the quotes coming from women.

Women also earn less than men, on average 14 per cent less for full-timers.[105] That's like women working without pay for the first seven weeks of the year. And it hasn't changed much in recent times: from 2001 to 2021, the gender pay gap narrowed by just 1 percentage point. The biggest gender pay gaps are to be found in the highest-paid occupations, such as professionals (25 per cent) and finance sector workers (24 per cent). By contrast, in the lower-paid occupation of public administration and safety, the gender pay gap is just 7 per cent, while among electricity, gas and waste workers, it's 8 per cent. The gender pay gap is mostly a story of glass ceilings, not sticky floors.

Recognising that the gender pay gap is largest among highly paid workers should not make us ignore gender inequity in manual labour jobs. But it is important to understand that gender inequity grows with wages, since it speaks to the challenge of tackling the problem. The gender pay gap has persisted despite the fact that women score higher than men on most exams and are more likely to complete high school. Fifty-five per cent of university students are female, with women comprising more than two-thirds of all students at some universities.

Some sceptics have argued that the gender pay gap is all a matter of choice, claiming that employers treat men and women equally. But that's not what people say in surveys. More women (23 per cent) than men (16 per cent) report having experienced sexual harassment at work in the previous twelve months.[106] Additional evidence comes from research which looked at what happens to wages when people undertake a gender transition using hormone therapy and surgery.[107] Average wages rise with female-to-male transitions and fall with male-to-female transitions.

While gender inequity is entrenched, it is not intractable. Right now, most high-status occupations demand a full-time commitment—there aren't many part-time neurosurgeons, judges or sharemarket traders. This means that these kinds of jobs are effectively off-limits to someone whose family commitments prevent them from working full-time. Creating more flexibility would disproportionately help women, who are more likely to take time to care for children or look after ageing parents. But it wouldn't hurt men, even those without caring responsibilities. A more flexible workplace also advantages employees who take time off for a sabbatical, to travel overseas, or to get better at their favourite sport.

Transparency also serves women well. Asking for a raise is a whole lot easier when you know what others are earning. In a male-dominated organisation, women may suffer from a lack of such knowledge and so be unable to press their case for fair remuneration. Insiders prefer secrecy, while outsiders benefit from transparency. A few years ago, it was revealed that Claire Foy, who played Queen Elizabeth II in the Netflix series *The Crown*, earned less than her co-star Matt Smith, who played Prince Philip. If the deal had been transparent, it's unlikely that the boys' club would have been able to underpay the actress. The same goes for Lisa Wilkinson, who left the TV chat show *Today* after it was revealed she was earning considerably less than co-host Karl Stefanovic.

One way of boosting transparency is to scrap pay-secrecy clauses that penalise employees from discussing their earnings with others. During a parliamentary hearing with Reserve Bank Governor Philip Lowe in 2021, I asked him whether his staff salary agreements included pay-secrecy clauses. After checking with his human resources department, Lowe was surprised to discover some of his staff were bound by such clauses. He immediately made a public pledge that the bank would not penalise employees who discussed their pay with co-workers. That's likely to most benefit the bank's female employees.

The gender pay gap is big at any single point in time, but it's even larger over a whole career. Take a 25-year-old man and a 25-year-old woman. If they each remain child-less, the man can expect to earn 5 per cent more over the course of a lifetime. Now imagine a 25-year-old man and woman who both decide to have children. In this case, the man can expect to earn almost twice as much as the woman over their lives.[108] Women can find themselves on the 'mummy track'.

In the world of sport, the old-fashioned view was that pregnancy was a career-ending event. But in recent decades, sports scientists have worked with female athletes to allow them to combine a successful athletic career with having a child. World champion marathoner Paula Radcliffe ran twice a day through the first five months of her pregnancy and was back running two weeks after giving birth. Less than a year later, she won the New York Marathon. Tennis player Serena Williams, cross-country skier Kikkan Randall and golfer Catriona Matthew are among the many women who have returned to the top of their sport after having a child. Coaches and sports administrators are getting better at supporting mothers who are elite athletes.

Parental leave sends a clear signal to women that society encourages them to combine work and family. It increases maternal attachment and raises breastfeeding rates. But by increasing the time that women spend out of the labour force, it may also increase the gender pay gap. Each year of maternity leave reduces women's earnings by up to 20 per cent.[109] The answer to this problem is not to scale back paid parental leave but rather to encourage fathers to take time off too.

It was in 1993 that the trailblazing Norwegian Government set aside a block of parental leave that could only be used by fathers—if a dad chooses not to take the allotted leave, it disappears. German fathers now get two 'daddy months', Swedish fathers get three months and French fathers get six months.[110] The consequence of these changes has been to significantly increase the amount of caring done by fathers.[111] Even after the leave period ends, these fathers generally spend more time at home and are more likely to help out around the house.[112] Fathers who take paternity leave are more likely to change nappies, bathe their babies and play with their children.[113]

Unfortunately, while the typical advanced nation provides two daddy months, our country only offers two *weeks*.[114] If child rearing was a global sport, other countries would be fielding teams with a much better gender balance than Australia.

Making jobs truly flexible, providing more pay transparency and giving fathers more paid leave are just some of the ways of closing the gender earnings gap. Efforts to eliminate discrimination and sexual harassment are critical too. What is at stake isn't just a fair go for the 51 per cent of the population who are women, but a more productive economy and a happier society.

EQUAL PLAY

On 17 April 1993, a few hours before their match was due to start, St Kilda footballers Nicky Winmar and Gilbert McAdam walked out of the visitors' locker room and strolled down the players' race to check out Victoria Park, then the home ground of rival team Collingwood. As soon as the Collingwood fans saw the two Indigenous players, the racial abuse began: 'Go and walkabout where you came from'; 'Go and sniff some petrol'.[115] Some especially venomous fans used what Winmar euphemistically called 'the black word'.

The pair decided they'd had enough. As Winmar recalls:

> We just looked at each other and, whether it was me or him, just basically said to each other, 'We're not going to put up with this crap! Let's get out there today and run amok. Let's get first and second best on ground.' And it was funny. It turned out that way and we won the game, which was the most important thing.[116]

St Kilda hadn't won at Victoria Park in seventeen years. When the game ended, Winmar was standing near the Collingwood cheer squad. He lifted up his guernsey, pointed to his skin and declared: 'I'm black. And I'm proud to be black!'

Some of the greatest moments in Australian sport have dealt with race. In 1968 in Mexico City, Australian sprinter Peter Norman won second place in the Olympic 200-metre race, in a time that still stands as the national record. Before the medal ceremony, the gold and bronze medallists, Tommie Smith and John Carlos, told Norman that they planned to raise their fists during the playing of the US national anthem. Norman told them, 'I'll stand with you.' All three wore Olympic Project for Human Rights badges, drawing attention to the campaign for civil rights in the United States.

Upon his return to Australia, Peter Norman was shunned by some, but others were keen to hear his story. My grandfather, Keith Leigh, was then the minister at Rosanna Methodist Church. Despite the fact that Norman was a devout member of the Salvation Army, my grandfather invited him to speak from the pulpit about racial equality and the events in Mexico City. Four decades later, in 2012, I moved a motion that the national parliament apologise posthumously to Peter Norman for the way he was treated after the 1968 Olympics. The apology was carried unanimously.

Over the past decade, athletes have protested both on-field and off-field racism. Nine years ago, during the AFL's Indigenous round, a thirteen-year-old Collingwood fan called Sydney player and dual Brownlow medallist Adam Goodes an 'ape'. Goodes later said that at that moment he had 'never been more hurt'. He pointed the girl out to security, who ejected her from the stadium. After the girl phoned him to apologise, Goodes was gracious: 'She's thirteen years old, still so innocent. I don't put any blame on her. Unfortunately it's what she hears, and the environment that she's grown up in has made her think that it's OK to call people names.'[117]

A few years later, to draw attention to racial inequity and police brutality, San Francisco 49ers quarterback Colin Kaepernick began kneeling instead of standing during the playing of the US national anthem. Through 2016 and 2017, the protests spread across America's National Football League and the soccer and baseball leagues. 'Taking a Knee' dovetailed with the Black Lives Matter movement, and the anthem protests won the support of major companies such as Ford, Under Armor and Nike. In response to a social media backlash from conservatives who publicly cut up or burned their Nike clothing, the company released a tongue-in-cheek advertisement explaining how to safely burn their products. The movement became so widespread that, in 2021, South African cricketer Quinton de Kock was chastised by his country's cricket authorities for *failing* to join his teammates in kneeling at the start of the game.

As with racism, sport has been at the cutting edge of public debate around homophobia. In Australia, Rugby League star Ian Roberts helped transform attitudes towards gay athletes. Described at age twenty-one as 'the best front rower in the game', he was both big and fast.[118] As a fellow player put it, Roberts 'could jump through the air and catch the ball like Superman, he could attack, he could defend and give you 40 tackles a game'.[119] His teammates knew he was gay, but most fans did not. That was until Roberts came out via a cover story in *New Weekly* magazine, which hit newsstands on 9 October 1995. He instantly became the most prominent gay sports star in Australia. The vitriol subsequently directed at Roberts was horrendous. The player dubbed 'the toughest man in Rugby League' was called a 'faggot' by one spectator. He was assaulted by two thugs while walking on the Sydney Harbour foreshore. But, as the first Rugby League player to come out as gay, Roberts played a powerful role in shaping attitudes towards homosexuality. According to one account, an old-timer on Manly's football committee reacted to the news by saying, 'Gee, given the way Roberts plays, maybe we should get a few more of those blokes on contract!'[120] Later reflecting on his decision, Roberts did not regret coming out when he did—indeed, he wished he had come out earlier.

Perhaps the area in which sport has done the most to change attitudes towards marginalised people is the Paralympics. After World War II, Britain established the 1948 International Wheelchair Games (also known as the Stoke Mandeville Games) for injured veterans to compete against one another. These competitions were eventually opened to non-veterans, and in 1960 the first Paralympics was held. The event shows people with disabilities as impressive individuals, not people to be pitied. Egyptian table tennis player Ibrahim Hamadtou lost both his arms after being run over by a train. He holds the paddle in his mouth and flicks the ball in the air with his foot to serve. His style of play has earned him the title 'Mr Impossible'. British athlete Sarah Storey was born without a functioning left hand. At age fourteen, she won her first Paralympic medal in swimming. She would go on to win twenty-seven more Paralympic medals over the next thirty years, switching to cycling when an ear infection brought an end to her swimming career. Storey has held seventy-five world records, and she broke another in 2021 on her way to winning gold at the age of forty-four.

The Paralympian I know best is Australian Kurt Fearnley, who has won pretty much every marathon wheelchair race in the world. At his peak, Fearnley would train using oxygen-deprivation equipment to simulate altitude. He's crawled the Kokoda Track, getting so many scratches on his body that he had to be bathed in antiseptic at the end of each day. Kurt Fearnley doesn't ask for pity— he demands respect.

Alas, many outcomes for Australians with disabilities still lag. People with disabilities are twice as likely to be unemployed, four times as likely to experience psychological distress, and significantly more likely to be poor.[121] The National Disability Insurance Scheme has helped, but Australia still trails many other countries regarding the share of people with disabilities who have a job. More employers need to see job applicants with disabilities the way we view Paralympians: in terms of their strengths and abilities, not their limitations and weaknesses.

When I was an economics professor, I worked with two colleagues to study racism in the labour market.[122] After receiving ethics approval from our university, we sent out over 4000 fake applications for waitstaff, customer service, data entry and sales jobs. The applications had similar résumés. The key difference was the name at the top, which had five variations: traditional Anglo (e.g., Jennifer Adams), Italian (Maria Romano), Indigenous (Betty Japanangka), Middle Eastern (Ahmed Baghdadi) and Chinese (Hong Lin). When the results came back, it was clear that having a non-Anglo name was costly in the labour market. To get as many job callbacks as an Anglo candidate, Italians had to send 12 per cent more applications, Indigenous people 35 per cent more, Middle Easterners 64 per cent more and Chinese people 68 per cent more. Disappointingly, we found little evidence that discrimination in hiring had dropped from levels reported in a similar study in the 1980s.

We had hoped our findings would cause employers to change their behaviour, but many minorities have found it easier to change their names. Muslim actor Moustafa Dennawi applied for dozens of jobs through a casting website and got zero replies. The day after changing his name to Tyler De Nawi, the responses started coming in—not just replies, but direct approaches. He notes the irony in the name Mustafa meaning 'the chosen one', adding: 'but it feels like changing my name was the only thing that would allow me to pursue my chosen path'.[123]

One solution to this issue is blind recruiting, which encourages employers to focus on the skills necessary to do the job. At its simplest, this can be achieved by removing from each résumé the candidate's name and any other information that might designate their gender or cultural background. A more comprehensive approach, championed by recruitment-software company Applied, is to dispense with résumés and instead invite candidates to apply through web platforms that ask specific questions about the requirements of the job.

What's so good about diversity? In innovative share-trading experiments, participants were asked to calculate accurate prices for simulated stocks, then trade them with others. This required the ability to reassess as new evidence emerged. It turned out that when participants were in diverse groups, their answers were more accurate and the markets were less prone to wild price gyrations.[124] The researchers who ran the experiments concluded that, when people were surrounded by others like them, errors were more likely to persist. Ethnic diversity was 'like fresh air', disrupting conformity and encouraging great performance.[125] Research also shows that, on the sporting field, diverse teams win more often.[126]

Surveys show that Australians have strongly negative views towards certain nationalities.[127] Just 6–7 per cent have a negative view of British, Italians and Germans, but 28 per cent have a negative view about Indians and 47 per cent have a negative view about Chinese people. While 11 per cent have a negative view about Christians, 37 per cent have a negative view about Muslims. Across our population, 24 per cent of Australians have a non-European or Indigenous background, yet on television, only 6 per cent of presenters, commentators and reporters have either an Indigenous or non-European background.[128] No person of colour has ever been appointed to the High Court of Australia.[129]

Despite the clear evidence of prejudice and under-representation of minorities, one marker of progress comes from differences across age groups. Younger Australians are much less likely to express prejudice against people of other nationalities, and almost unanimously agree that 'multiculturalism has been good for Australia'. The same holds for attitudes to sexuality. In surveys of the general population, only around 3–4 per cent of people say that they are bisexual, gay or lesbian. But in a recent survey of secondary schoolers, 21 per cent of students in years 10, 11 and 12 said they were homosexual or bisexual.[130] As the marriage equality plebiscite demonstrated, LGBTIQ+ attitudes in the population have shifted dramatically over a generation, with young people leading the way. Attitudes towards transgender people are evolving too. Still, sexuality appears to matter in the labour market: on average, gay men earn less than straight men, while lesbian women earn more than straight women.[131]

One way in which sport can help reduce these barriers is by establishing institutions that carry a team's prestige. In Townsville, NRL Cowboys House provides accommodation to more than 100 young Indigenous men and women, allowing them to attend high-quality schools. Most of the students are from remote Queensland communities which lack the established secondary school options available in Townsville. Cowboys players regularly visit to mentor and motivate students. A key to the success of the facility is that the North Queensland Cowboys are trusted by Indigenous families. As one of the managers of Cowboys House pointed out to me when I visited, the NRL team is more likely to be trusted than the state or federal government, so their brand allows them to achieve more than governments can.

A hybrid model is Rob de Castella's Indigenous Marathon Foundation, a six-month program that uses marathon training as a means of fostering leadership skills among a dozen Indigenous men and women. The athletic training is accompanied by a physical education qualification and opportunities for public speaking. Each participant runs a marathon, but the race is a means to self-improvement, not simply a sporting accomplishment.

Corporate Australia is recognising that it has a long way to go before its offices are as ethnically and racially diverse as the nation's playing fields. To address the problem, firms have begun to better evaluate which programs work and which do not. Despite the popularity of unconscious bias training, a systematic review found that most programs had little effect on racial and ethnic attitudes.[132] In some cases, diversity workshops have even made the problem worse—perhaps because they reinforce stereotypes or provoke a backlash.[133] Working with managers for multiple months has a bigger impact than a one-day training session.[134] To anyone who's ever prepared for a sporting event, this should not be surprising: change takes time.

Australia's approach to race and ethnicity goes to the heart of our national identity. It involves recognising that the nation stands at the confluence of three powerful rivers. Indigenous Australians have occupied this land for at least 65 000 years, a period that predates human settlement of Europe and the Americas. All Australians can take pride in sharing a continent with a people whose civilisation had been around for tens of thousands of years before ancient Greece and ancient Rome. The second source of identity comes from the British institutions that underpin our legal system and market economy. No other nation has shaped Australia more than the United Kingdom, and our story is incomplete if it ignores the history of colonialism, shared sacrifice in war, and a common culture. The third river is multiculturalism, which has seen Australia successfully integrate a higher share of migrants than virtually any other advanced nation.

At last year's Tokyo Olympics, these influences were showcased by an Australian squad that comprised 3 per cent Indigenous athletes and 14 per cent athletes born overseas, and in which the predominant ancestry was British. Yet there is more work to be done. As Aboriginal leader Noel Pearson observes, constitutional recognition of Indigenous Australians would be a powerful way of uniting these three parts of our national identity, making Australia 'a more complete commonwealth'.[135]

ENDGAME

Sport is a source of personal pleasure and national pride. Team sports reflect a unity of purpose and the strength of diversity. Athletes remind us that sacrifice, courage and kindness are not outdated values but admirable traits in the modern world. Sport is imperfect, yet at its best, it uplifts and inspires.

Building a fairer society is a team sport, as is creating a stronger economy. There is no single solution to our social and economic problems, but the right set of ideas can work magic. Like sporting talent scouts, Australia needs to become better at nurturing entrepreneurs from unconventional backgrounds. We need to encourage dynamic markets by curbing monopoly power. To ensure workers are fairly paid, it's vital that they can move between organisations and be represented by strong unions. Curbing the mistreatment of hospitality workers, defending penalty rates and providing universal sick leave will help restore the dignity of work. And just imagine how much more sport we could watch with a couple more weeks' annual leave.

Just as great players rely on their coaches, education is vital to building a happier and healthier society. Attracting and retaining great school teachers is perhaps the best single thing we could do to create a more affluent and equitable society. The advances of technology shouldn't lead us to give up on work any more than the rise of fast food should lead us to yield in the battle against obesity and inactivity. Wage subsidies and job-creation programs can be targeted at those who are out of work. Managers can also do more to prevent email turning employees into human network routers, and make work more meaningful.

Sport has often led the national conversation on inclusion, proving that more diverse teams can kick more goals. Better reporting of the problems, and better evaluation of the solutions, can help companies benefit from racial and ethnic diversity. Likewise regarding gender diversity, where eliminating sexual harassment, making jobs more flexible and encouraging dads to take parental leave can help narrow the gap.

When the final whistle blows, sport reminds us that life is rarely a choice between fairness and excellence. Sportspeople who play hard but treat their opponents with grace are the ones we honour with statues, speeches and best-and-fairest trophies. On the field or court or track, successful athletes are strong and generous, tough and inclusive. Let's make our society and our economy a fair game too.

ACKNOWLEDGEMENTS

This book was written in Canberra, on the traditional lands of the Ngunnawal people. I pay my respect to their Elders and to Indigenous leaders across Australia.

Much of my thinking about equity and efficiency was shaped by my co-author Tony Atkinson. He was a remarkable scholar: passionate about the issues, meticulous about the facts. One of my fondest memories of his final years is walking together across the Oxford playing fields while discussing social justice.

Special thanks to Stephanie Anderson, James Button, Rob de Castella, Graham Evans, Peter FitzSimons, Martin Flanagan, Tim Gavel, Dennis Glover, Gideon Haigh, Barbara Leigh, Michael Leigh, Jennifer Rayner and Nick Terrell for conversations and feedback on early drafts; Srinivas Manchikanti for some early exploratory research; and Louise Adler, Paul Smitz and the Monash University Publishing team for their deft work on, and timely production of, this book. I am indebted to Adam Triggs, who allowed me to use our co-authored work on competition.

My Labor colleagues are passionate pro-growth progressives who have taught me a great deal about sport and social change in communities across Australia. In recent years, I've co-founded the Parliamentary Friends of Cycling and the Parliamentary Friends of Running, which help promote those sports while doing our bit for bipartisanship.

Finally, this book is dedicated to my extraordinary wife Gweneth and our three children: Zachary, Theodore and Sebastian. Thank you for tolerating my time-consuming exercise pursuits, and for your insights as this project unfolded. My love for each of you knows no finish line.

NOTES

1   Peter FitzSimons, *Everyone but Phar Lap: Face to Face with the Best of Australian Sport*, HarperCollins, Sydney, 1997, pp. 40–5.

2   Marion Stell, *Half the Race: A History of Australian Women in Sport*, HarperCollins, Sydney, 1991, p. 237.

3   Andrew Leigh, *Battlers and Billionaires: The Story of Inequality in Australia*, Black Inc., Melbourne, 2013, p. 47; stats updated to 2021 from Australian Bureau of Statistics (ABS), 'Employee Earnings and Hours'. The lowest-paid and highest-paid are the tenth and ninetieth percentiles, respectively.

4   Andrew Leigh and Nick Terrell, *Reconnected: A Community Builder's Handbook*, Black Inc., Melbourne, 2020.

5   Ibid.

6   Jordan Baker and Rosie King, 'How We've Grown: Average Aussie Women Two Dress Sizes Bigger than in 1966', *Daily Telegraph*, 28 February 2016.

7   Brooklyn J Fraser et al., 'The Great Leap Backward: Changes in the Jumping Performance of Australian Children Aged 11–12-years between 1985 and 2015', *Journal of Sports Sciences*, vol. 37, no. 7, 2019, pp. 748–54.

8   Joachim Hüffmeier and Guido Hertel, 'When the Whole Is More than the Sum of Its Parts: Group Motivation Gains in the Wild', *Journal of Experimental Social Psychology*, vol. 47, no. 2, 2011, pp. 455–9.

9   Richard Cashman and Amanda Weaver, *Wicket Women: Cricket and Women in Australia*, New South Wales University Press, Sydney, 1991, p. 13.

10 Productivity Commission, 'PC Productivity Insights: Australia's Long Term Productivity Experience', Canberra, November 2020.

11 Productivity Commission, 'PC Productivity Insights: Recent Productivity Trends', Canberra, February 2020, p. 6.

12 Productivity Commission, 'PC Productivity Insights: Recent Developments,' Canberra, June 2021, p. 3. The comparison holds even if we exclude the COVID pandemic.

13 Dan Andrews et al., 'Reaching for the Stars: Australian Firms and the Global Productivity Frontier', Working Paper 2022-1, Treasury, Canberra, 2022.

14 Omer Majeed et al., 'What Drives High Growth? Characteristics of Australian Firms', *Economic Record*, vol. 97, no. 318, 2021, pp. 350–64.

15 Sasan Bakhtiari, 'Entrepreneurship Dynamics in Australia: Lessons from Micro-data', *Economic Record*, vol. 95, no. 308, 2019, pp. 114–40.

16 Owen Slot, Simon Timson and Chelsea Warr, *The Talent Lab: The Secret to Finding, Creating and Sustaining Success*, Random House, New York, 2017.

17 Alex Bell et al., 'Who Becomes an Inventor in America? The Importance of Exposure to Innovation', *Quarterly Journal of Economics*, vol. 134, no. 2, 2019, pp. 647–713.

18 Startup Muster, '2018 Startup Muster Annual Report', Sydney, 2019.

19 Dan Andrews et al., 'Wage Growth in Australia: Lessons from Longitudinal Microdata', Working Paper 2019-04, Treasury, Canberra, 2019.

20 Annual interstate migration data sourced from ABS, 'Australian Historical Population Statistics', cat. no. 3105.0.65.001.

21 Census figures show that the share of people who moved house was 39.4 per cent in 1966–71 but 38.9 per cent in 2011–16.

22 This analysis is based on market capitalisation: 1986 firms from Business Council of Australia, 'Living on Borrowed Time: Australia's Economic Future', Discussion Paper, BCA, Melbourne, 2021.

23 Thomas Mathews, 'A History of Australian Equities', Research Discussion Paper 2019-04, Reserve Bank of Australia, Sydney, 2019, updated by RBA, 'Background on the Australian Listed Equity Market', submission to the House of Representatives Standing Committee on Economics Inquiry into Common Ownership and Capital Concentration in Australia, 2021.

24 Cal Newport, *A World without Email: Reimagining Work in an Age of Communication Overload*, Penguin, New York, 2021.

25 Jiri Dvorak et al., 'Football Is the Most Popular Sport Worldwide', *American Journal of Sports Medicine*, vol. 32, suppl. 1, 2004, pp. 3S–4S.

26 George Megalogenis, *The Football Solution: How Richmond's Premiership Can Save Australia*, Penguin, Sydney, 2018, p. 8.

27 This section draws on Andrew Leigh and Adam Triggs, 'A Few Big Firms', *The Monthly* (online), 17 May 2017.

28 Luigi Zingales, *A Capitalism for the People: Recapturing the Lost Genius of American Prosperity*, Basic Books, New York, 2014, p. 31.

29 Sandra Black and Philip Strahan, 'The Division of Spoils: Rent-Sharing and Discrimination in a Regulated Industry', *American Economic Review*, vol. 91, no. 4, 2001, pp. 814–31.

30 Orn Bodvarsson and Shawn Pettman, 'Racial Wage Discrimination in Major League Baseball: Do Free Agency and League Size Matter?', *Applied Economics Letters*, vol. 9, no. 12, 2002, pp. 791–6.

31 Andrew Leigh and Adam Triggs, 'Markets, Monopolies and Moguls: The Relationship between Inequality and Competition', *Australian Economic Review*, vol. 49, no. 4, 2016, pp. 389–412.

32 John Siegfried and David Round, 'How Did the Wealthiest Australians Get So Rich?', *Review of Income and Wealth*, vol. 40, no. 2, 1994, pp. 191–204.

33 In 1989, there were 259 mergers in Australia, with a combined value of US$34 billion. In 2020, there were 1671 mergers, with a combined value of US$372 billion: see https://imaa-institute.org/

34 Leigh and Triggs, 'Markets, Monopolies and Moguls'.

35 Rod Sims, 'Protecting and Promoting Competition in Australia', speech, 27 August 2021.

36 David Williamson, *Home Truths: A Memoir*, HarperCollins, Sydney, 2021, p. 229.

37 Sims, 'Protecting and Promoting Competition'.

38 'For the Record: McEnroe's Tantrums and Fines', *Deseret News*, 4 July 1991.

39 Tony Collins, *How Football Began: A Global History of How the World's Football Codes Were Born*, Routledge, New York, 2018, p. 140.

40 Keith Dunstan, *Sports*, Cassell Australia, Melbourne, 1973, p. 237.

41 Douglas Booth and Colin Tatz, *One-Eyed: A View of Australian Sport*, Allen & Unwin, Sydney, 2000, p. 58.

42 'Dr. H. V. Evatt', *Canberra Times*, 19 December 1930, p. 1.

43 Booth and Tatz, *One-Eyed*, p. 145.

44 Greg Jericho and Gareth Hutchens, 'Whatever Happened to Wage Rises in Australia?', *Guardian*, 28 February 2018.

45 Jim Stanford, 'The Declining Labour Share in Australia: Definition, Measurement, and International Comparisons', *Journal of Australian Political Economy*, no. 81, winter 2018, pp. 11–32.

46 Gareth Hutchens, 'Why Company Profits Have Jumped in Australia During COVID-19 While Workers Are Taking Home Less', *ABC Online*, 3 September 2020.

47 Lexi Metherell, 'Fair Work Ombudsman Ill-Equipped to Handle Migrant Worker Claims: Researchers', *AM*, 29 October 2018.

48 Patrick Laplange, Maurice Glover and Tim Fry, 'The Growth of Labour Hire Employment in Australia', Productivity Commission, Melbourne, 2005; ABS, 'Characteristics of Employment, August 2016', cat. no. 6333.0, 2017.

49 Senate Select Committee on Job Security, *First Interim Report: On-Demand Platform Work in Australia*, Canberra, 2021, p. 88.

50 See Kronos, 'Workforce Forecast Manager', https://www.kronos.com.au/products/workforce-central-suite/workforce-forecast-manager

51 Cody Atkinson and Sean Lawson, 'How the Re-Introduction of Free Agency Has Changed the AFL', *ABC Online*, 13 October 2021.

52 Alejandro Donado, 'How Trade Unions Increase Welfare', *Economic Journal*, vol. 122, no. 563, 2012, pp. 990–1009; Lixin Cai and Amy YC Liu, 'Union Wage Effects in Australia: Is There Variation along the Distribution?', *Economic Record*, vol. 84, no. 267, 2008, pp. 496–510.

53 FitzSimons, *Everyone but Phar Lap*, pp. 50–4.

54 Ibid., pp. 40–5.

55 Ibid., pp. 2–3.

56 Ibid., pp. 36–8.

57 This survey figure and the quote are drawn from the Shop, Distributive and Allied Employees Association's background materials for its 'No-one Deserves a Serve' campaign.

58 Daniel Schneider and Kristen Harknett, 'Consequences of Routine Work-Schedule Instability for Worker Health and Well-Being', *American Sociological Review*, vol. 84, no. 1, 2019, pp. 82–114.

59 Thomas Crawley, 'The Effect of Weekend Work on Shared Leisure Time', *Australian Economic Review*, vol. 54, no. 3, 2021, pp. 406–15.

60 Michael Huberman and Chris Minns, 'The Times They Are Not Changin': Days and Hours of Work in Old and New Worlds, 1870–2000', *Explorations in Economic History*, vol. 44, no. 4, 2007, pp. 538–67.

61 John Maynard Keynes, 'Economic Possibilities for Our Grandchildren', in *Essays in Persuasion*, Palgrave Macmillan, London, 2010 [1930], pp. 321–32.

62 Grant Cairncross and Iain Waller, 'Not Taking Annual Leave: What Could It Cost Australia?', *Journal of Economic and Social Policy*, vol. 9, no. 1, 2004, article 3.

63 Richard Denniss, 'Annual Leave in Australia: An Analysis of Entitlements, Usage and Preferences', Discussion Paper 56, Australia Institute, Canberra, 2003.

64 Erica Scharrer, 'Why Are Sitcom Dads Still So Inept?', *The Conversation*, 16 June 2020.

65 Michael Sandel, *The Tyranny of Merit: What's Become of the Common Good?*, Farrar, Straus and Giroux, New York, 2020; Jon Cruddas, *The Dignity of Labour*, Polity, London, 2021.

66 Martin Luther King Jr, speech to striking sanitation workers, Memphis, TN, 18 March 1968.

67 This section draws in part on Andrew Leigh, 'Schooled: How Australia Dropped the Ball on Education, and How We Can Recover', *Griffith Review*, no. 75, 2022, pp. 34–46.

68 Veronica Allan, 'The Surprising Role of Childhood Trauma in Athletic Success', *The Conversation*, 10 December 2018.

69 This account from Mick Colliss, *Australia's Toughest Sportspeople: Twelve Athletes Who Epitomise the Grit, Courage and Determination of Australian Sport*, Affirm Press, Melbourne, 2021, pp. 23–59.

70 FitzSimons, *Everyone but Phar Lap*, p. 127.

71 World Athletics, 'Golden Dawn for Cathy Freeman', 9 January 1998.

72 Lance Lochner, 'Nonproduction Benefits of Education: Crime, Health, and Good Citizenship', in Eric Hanushek, Stephen Machin and Ludger Woessmann (eds), *Handbook of the Economics of Education*, vol. 4, ch. 2, Elsevier Science, Amsterdam, 2011, pp. 183–282.

73 Andrew Leigh, 'Returns to Education in Australia', *Economic Papers: A Journal of Applied Economics and Policy*, vol. 27, no. 3, 2008, pp. 233–49.

74 Andrew Norton and Ittima Cherastidtham, 'Risks and Rewards: When Is Vocational Education a Good Alternative to Higher Education?', Grattan Institute, Melbourne, 2019.

75 Sue Thomson et al., *PISA 2018: Reporting Australia's Results—Volume I: Student Performance*, ACER, Melbourne, 2019, pp. 32, 112, 176.

76 Andrew Leigh, 'Estimating Teacher Effectiveness from Two-Year Changes in Students' Test Scores', *Economics of Education Review*, vol. 29, no. 3, 2010, pp. 480–8.

77 Andrew Leigh and Chris Ryan, 'How and Why Has Teacher Quality Changed in Australia?', *Australian Economic Review*, vol. 41, no. 2, 2008, pp. 141–59; Julie Sonnemann, 'We Need to Attract More High Achievers to Teaching', Grattan Institute, Melbourne, 2021.

78 Joshua Gans and Andrew Leigh, *Innovation + Equality: How to Create a Future that Is More Star Trek than Terminator*, MIT Press, Cambridge, MA, 2019.

79 NCVER, 'Historical Time Series of Apprenticeships and Traineeships in Australia', Adelaide, 2020.

80 NCVER, 'Latest VET Completion Rates Now Available', media release, 1 December 2020.

81 Andrew Norton, 'Demand-Driven Funding for Universities Is Frozen: What Does This Mean and Should the Policy Be Restored?', *The Conversation*, 2 May 2019.

82 Universities Australia, 'Higher Education: Facts and Figures', Canberra, 2020.

83 Andrew Leigh, 'Australian Mobility Report Cards: Which Universities Admit the Most Disadvantaged Students?', *Australian Economic Review*, vol. 54, no. 3, 2021, pp. 331–42.

84 Bonnie Tsui, *Why We Swim*, Workman Publishing, New York, 2021, p. 6.

85 Henry David Thoreau, *Walden and Other Writings*, Bantam Books, New York, 1981 [1854], p. 171.

86 Christopher McDougall, *Born to Run: A Hidden Tribe, Superathletes, and the Greatest Race the World Has Never Seen*, Knopf, New York, 2009, p. 93.

87 Haruki Murakami, *What I Talk about When I Talk about Running*, Knopf, New York, 2008, p. 95.

88 Jean Bobet, *Tomorrow, We Ride*, Mousehold Press, Norwich, 2008, p. 113.

89 Michael Coelli and Jeff Borland, 'Job Polarisation and Earnings Inequality in Australia', *Economic Record*, vol. 92, no. 296, 2016, pp. 1–27; Roger Wilkins and Mark Wooden, 'Two Decades of Change: The Australian Labour Market, 1993–2013', *Australian Economic Review*, vol. 47, no. 4, 2014, pp. 417–31.

90 Glenn Stevens, 'The Challenge of Prosperity', CEDA, Melbourne, 29 November 2010.

91 Nick Carroll, 'Unemployment and Psychological Well-Being', *Economic Record*, vol. 83, no. 262, 2007, pp. 287–302.

92 Robert Breunig and Timothy Watson, 'Strengthening JobKeeper: Reviewing the Government's Flagship Stimulus Program', *Policy Forum*, 16 June 2020.

93 Stell, *Half the Race*, p. 103.

94 Cashman and Weaver, *Wicket Women*, p. 28.

95 Stell, *Half the Race*, p. 24.

96 Brunette Lenkić and Rob Hess, *Play On! The Hidden History of Women's Australian Rules Football*, Echo, Richmond, Vic., 2016, p. 4.

97 As recounted on her website: see https://kathrineswitzer.com

98 Figures are available at https://www.baa.org

99 Jay Coakley et al., *Sports in Society: Issues and Controversies in Australia and New Zealand*, McGraw Hill, Sydney, 2009, p. 258.

100 Talya Minsberg, 'Games Strive for Gender Equity, but Equality Still Seems Far Off', *New York Times*, 23 July 2021, p. B10.

101 Quoted in Angela Pippos, *Breaking the Mould*, Affirm Press, Melbourne, 2017, p. 222.

102 Watermark Search International, '2021 Board Diversity Index', Sydney; CEW, 'CEW Senior Executive Census 2021', 2021.

103 Tracey Spicer, 'Why Aren't More Women Immortalised in Stone?', *Sydney Morning Herald*, 29 September 2017.

104 Jenna Price and Blair Williams, '2021 Women for Media Report: "Take the Next Steps"', Women's Leadership Institute Australia, Melbourne, 2021.

105 WGEA, 'Australia's Gender Pay Gap Statistics', 27 August 2021.

106 Australian Human Rights Commission, *Everyone's Business: Fourth National Survey on Sexual Harassment in Australian Workplaces*, Sydney, 2018.

107 Kristen Schilt and Matthew Wiswall, 'Before and After: Gender Transitions, Human Capital, and Workplace Experiences', *BE Journal of Economic Analysis & Policy*, vol. 8, no. 1, 2008, article 39.

108 Rebecca Cassells et al., *She Works Hard for the Money: Australian Women and the Gender Divide*, NATSEM, Canberra, 2009, p. 32.

109 *The Economist*, 'A Father's Place', 16 May 2015.

110 OECD Family Database, table PF2.1.B, 2020 (figures are the total of paid paternity leave plus paid parental and home care leave reserved for fathers).

111 *The Economist*, 'A Father's Place'; Ankita Patnaik, 'Reserving Time for Daddy: The Consequences of Fathers' Quotas', *Journal of Labor Economics*, vol. 37, no. 4, 2019, pp.1009–59; ILO, 'Modern Daddy: Norway's Progressive Policy on

Paternity Leave', *World of Work Magazine*, no. 54, 2005, pp. 12–15.

112 Patnaik, 'Reserving Time for Daddy'.

113 *The Economist*, 'The Dad Dividend', 16 May 2015.

114 OECD Family Database; Guyonne Kalb, 'Paid Parental Leave and Female Labour Supply: A Review', *Economic Record*, vol. 94, no. 304, 2018, pp. 80–100.

115 Danny Blay's recollections on https://www.saints.com.au, 27 June 2004.

116 Michael Gordon, 'The Day Winmar Drew the Line', *Canberra Times*, 17 April 2013, p. 23.

117 Jon Pierek and Deborah Gough, 'Goodes Accepts Apology for Teen's Slur', *Sydney Morning Herald*, 26 May 2013.

118 Tim Bauer, 'Atonement', *Good Weekend*, 30 January 2010, p. 17.

119 Patrick Skene, 'The Courageous Journey of Ian Roberts, Rugby League's First Openly Gay Player', *Guardian*, 18 August 2015.

120 Peter FitzSimons, *Everyone and Phar Lap: Face to Face with the Best of Australian Sport*, HarperCollins, Sydney, 1999, pp. 190–1.

121 AIHW, 'People with Disability in Australia 2020', Canberra, 2020.

122 Alison Booth, Andrew Leigh and Elena Varganova, 'Does Ethnic Discrimination Vary across Minority Groups? Evidence from a Field Experiment', *Oxford Bulletin of Economics and Statistics*, vol. 74, no. 4, 2012, pp. 547–73.

123 Tyler De Nawi, 'Breaking down the Barriers', *Canberra Times*, 21 May 2016, p. F3.

124 Sheen Levine et al., 'Ethnic Diversity Deflates Price Bubbles', *Proceedings of the National Academy of Sciences*, vol. 111, no. 52, 2014, pp. 18524–9.

125 Sheen Levine and David Stark, 'Diversity Makes You Brighter', *New York Times*, 9 December 2015, p. A35.

126 Woojun Lee and George Cunningham, 'Group Diversity's Influence on Sport Teams and Organizations: A Meta-Analytic Examination and Identification of Key Moderators', *European Sport Management Quarterly*, vol. 19, no. 2, 2019, pp. 139–59.

127 Andrew Markus, *Mapping Social Cohesion 2020*, Scanlon Foundation, Melbourne, 2021, pp. 6–7.

128 Media Diversity Australia, 'Who Gets To Tell Australian Stories?', Sydney, 2020.

129 Ray Steinwall, 'Colourful Justice: What Australia Must Learn from the US', *Proctor*, Queensland Law Society, Brisbane, 14 October 2021.

130 Christopher Fisher et al., *6th National Survey of Australian Secondary Students and Sexual Health 2018*, La Trobe University, Bundoora, Vic., 2019, p. 19.

131 Nick Drydakis, 'Sexual Orientation and Earnings: A Meta-Analysis 2012–2020', *Journal of Population Economics*, vol. 35, no. 2, 2022, pp. 409–40.

132 Patrick Forscher et al., 'A Meta-Analysis of Procedures to Change Implicit Measures', *Journal of Personality and Social Psychology*, vol. 117, no. 3, 2019, pp. 522–59.

133 Alexandra Kalev, Frank Dobbin and Erin Kelly, 'Best Practices or Best Guesses? Assessing the Efficacy of Corporate Affirmative Action and Diversity Policies', *American Sociological Review*, vol. 71, no. 4, 2006, pp. 589–617.

134 Francesca Gino and Katherine Coffman, 'Unconscious Bias Training that Works', *Harvard Business Review*, vol. 99, no. 5, 2021, pp. 114–23.

135 Noel Pearson, 'A Rightful Place: Race, Recognition and a More Complete Commonwealth', *Quarterly Essay* 55, Black Inc., Melbourne, 2014, p. 55.